# It's You NOW!

*7 Secrets to Living Life On Your Own Terms*

**SARAH RENEE LANGLEY, PhD, LPC**

**ISBN:** 978-0-9973341-0-4

**Disclaimer.** All the material contained in this book is provided for educational and informational purposes only. No responsibility can be taken for any results or outcomes resulting from the use of this material. While every attempt has been made to provide information that is both accurate and effective, the author does not assume any responsibility for the accuracy or use/misuse of this information.

**Thank You Gifts.** As a thank you for taking action and purchasing my book, please use this code and link to receive FREE downloadable exercises you will need with the book. Cheers!

http://sarahreneelangley.com/itsyourturnnow

# It's Your Turn NOW!

# Dedication

*This book is dedicated to all the LeadHERs who are successful in their own right, and now need to know that it's their turn now to live their lives to the fullest extent. On their own terms.*

*I also want to give a special dedication to my mom, Mrs. Mary Nelson Langley, who demonstrated true LeadHER qualities, and had given an incredible example to follow. Thank you Mom.*

*My final dedication is to God. This would not be possible if You hadn't intended for me to live my life on purpose. I intend to live my life the way You intended for me to live it, and to share my story and message to the world. Thank You God.*

*"When you learn, teach. When you get, give."*

**Maya Angelou**

# Contents

# Foreword

I want to tell you why I wrote this foreword. I am a best selling author, movie producer, investment banker economist, and Chairman Founder of the Forbes # 1 Entrepreneur Conference in the world. I resigned from CEO SPACE in 2013 and have stood for 30 years in Full Partnership with women in every opportunity imaginable. I placed my wife September as COO, elevating her to President and CEO of the organization. September and her lady leaders have taken CEO SPACE from # 5 on the top ten *Forbes List of Conferences a Business Owner cannot afford to miss*, to #1. I walk the walk and talk the talk in my service to the world as a role model for lady leaders.

I believe any male leader in the "C" Suites can appreciate that the largest buyer purchasing group on earth are women, and their leadership role from the Board to Public Office requires male education and understanding to acknowledge, recognize, and collaborate effectively with lady leaders around our global village. It's Your Turn Now is a required read for all women entrepreneurs and executives who want more success but are missing their ability to be happy in the process.

I wrote this foreword for another reason. I believe that the credentials, experience and break through protocols Dr. Sarah brings to the market are as important as other ground breaking products and services I have helped support over time. When I say ground breaking products and services, I mean Chicken Soup for the Soul, Men Are from Mars, Rich Dad Poor Dad, Outwitting the Devil, No Matter What by Lisa Nichols, Think and Grow Rich for Women by Sharon Lechter, and now It's Your Turn Now is the next best up and coming book on the planet! I watched these books unfold and break the Guinness Book of Records. It is time for It's Your Turn Now to come into the limelight and do what it's intended to do, which is to serve our women leaders.

Dr. Sarah has hit the lady leader objective dead center. She wishes to see Lady Leaders not only win and BE successful but to have an inner GPS inside in owning their significance and living their own lives in the highest potential and with a full and healthy self-esteem. Dr. Sarah pinpoints and identifies self-sabotaging behaviors that keep women stuck, and she personally shares how to get unstuck and move forward to happiness and success through her 7 secrets in It's Your Turn Now.

It's Your Turn Now defines principles we have lived for over 30 years at CEO Space International. It's Your Turn Now is like a living CEO Space in a book where you don't have to invest thousands of dollars or do a ten-day spiritual retreat to find yourself. What you are seeking after is in this book.

It's Your Turn Now reads you while you read It's Your Turn Now. Trust me on this one ladies, you will want to have highlighters and a pen while you read. You will pinpoint phrases that you can use in management and leadership trainings. Make notes in the book of future things to do, and make a list of what you are committing to do to make it your turn Now. It's Your Turn Now will accelerate your success and happiness by going about it the correct way, which is starting by working on you first. Think of It's Your Turn Now as the magical GPS for lady leaders accelerating in speed while driving on their journey of happiness and success. It's Your Turn Now is the double lines that keep you from hitting the curb along the way. It's Your Turn is the voice in your head telling you to make your U turn to your own true happiness so that you don't miss the up ramp to substantial success. All who reads this book will profit and benefit from the secrets and wisdom Dr. Sarah provides in It's Your Turn Now.

I am strongly encouraging you to get 10 It's Your Turn Now books, never less than 5, and keep inventory so you can share with all of your customers and alliance partners and suppliers where women are involved. You will retain your existing customers by gifting them It's Your Turn Now, and will obtain greater repeat sales and referrals because as you give so shall you receive. Give the gift that transforms lady leaders everywhere that will inspire them to take their turn Now.

It's Your Turn Now tackles the core inner compass that resides within. In this book, Dr. Sarah challenges the questions marks that resonates in many minds, "Am I doing this work as a legacy for some one else? What do I wish to do so that my life absolutely thrills me?" Dr. Sarah helps you begin the process to start including yourself in the equation without guilt, worry, or apology. Through It's Your Turn NOW, Dr. Sarah helps you learn how to have real conversations with yourself about your life, encourages you to ask the hard questions about where you are right now, if you are happy, and what success truly means to you. She also empowers you to seek your *Why*, or in other words, to seek your true authentic self, your true calling, and the reason of your existence.

I ask everyone to leave comments and feedback which creates a global best seller if you feel like I do as you read the sacred inspired words within It's Your Turn Now.

If I don't stop, I'll write a book about the book. I haven't been this turned on and switched on to this magnitude. Thanks Sarah! I see that It's Your Turn Now is a work of divine appointment that is an answer to prayers everywhere!

I'm Berny Dohrmann and I so approve this message.

Berny Dohrmann
Chairman, CEO Space International

# Preface

Are you ready to make a difference? Are you ready to move away from the darkness and into the light? Are you ready to be fulfilled rather than broken from the inside? Are you ready to be happy with your life without any apologetic feelings or guilt? Are you ready? It's your turn to be happy and successful. There will be challenges along the way, which you already know, but it will be well worth it in the end.

What's holding you back? What is it that you have been depending on for so long that keeps you stuck or comfortable? What has you continually doing the same thing and expecting different results? It's understandable that what you have done in the past worked and produced great success, but at who's expense and at what cost? How did it really benefit you? Are you truly happy? Please be honest with yourself. If you are happy, great! If you are not, let's address it. It is time for you to be happy and make the proper moves in achieving something worthwhile for you *Right Now*.

## It's Your Turn NOW!

There may have been times in your life that you wanted to scream, but were too afraid that others would hear you and discover how stressed out, burned out, and maxed out you really are in trying to keep your lifestyle up for the sake of pleasing everyone or maintaining status quo. You may suffer from the imposter syndrome, believing that you are not what you make yourself out to be to everyone. You may even think if anyone finds out who you really are, it may not only jeopardize all that you have worked hard for, but it would also grossly impact the livelihood of those you care about and are responsible for. So instead, you choose to suffer in silence.

Amazingly, this is the life that most women live. It is sad. The passion, determination and drive to be successful is often driven by some type of motivation that doesn't have really much to do with them. Many women convince themselves that they do benefit in some way, and there are benefits, but the sacrifices are mostly, if not entirely, at their expense. Why? Who said you had to give up on your dreams and desires? Who said you couldn't have both? You know how to be passionate and driven to take matters into your own hands when it comes to your family, job, and money, now let's direct that same passion and drive towards doing what makes you truly happy and what truly benefits you. And, it's ok it if only and solely benefits you for a change.

Before we begin, may I ask you a questions? Do you even know what makes you happy? If you do not, it's ok. I will help you discover your happiness in this book.

First, I want you to tap into a life long desire or vision you once had a long time ago. You thought you may have buried it, but that desire or vision keeps gnawing at you to this day. It is ok, I give you permission to now take the time to explore and acknowledge what that dream or vision is saying to you. I will show you how to give yourself permission on many levels so that you don't feel stuck or powerless in things that you want to do that others may not agree. I encourage you to set this goal in giving yourself permission to do the things you dream and desire to do, in order to embark on a new journey of taking your turn and living life on your own terms. You may feel like you have been living your life on other people's terms and wondered when it would be your turn to call the shots on your own life. I am saying to you, It's Your Turn, Now. Take it!

It is also time for you to push pause on the dreams and visions others have for you. From reading this book you may discover that you are doing things that others you love have done in the past. You may be managing the family business as a way to appease your parents. Your life long mission may be to make them happy so they can be proud of you and can finally recognize your importance and worth. Yet, you're still not happy because you think that what you do may never be enough to please them. And as a result, you interpret that you aren't good enough. This keeps the vicious cycle going in other areas in your life because *how you do one thing is how you do everything.*

I wonder if you daydream what life would have been like if you had made that left turn in the fork of the road instead of listening to everyone else telling you to make the right turn? I wonder if you are at a place in your life that, while you are successful, you feel empty, unfulfilled, and incomplete? Is it because all your life you had lived on other people's terms instead of your own terms?

I understand. I have been there. This is the reason I have decided to write this book for you. I will share later in the book what it was like for me living on other people's terms, and how I quickly changed all that. For now I am declaring, *It's your turn Now! It's your turn to live life on your own terms, guiltlessly and unapologetically!* You have fulfilled your duties and responsibilities. Who says you can't pursue your own happiness and still attend to your obligations? Please stop trying to convince yourself that you are happy and successful because you have a family, good career, good job, and money to show for it! Please own up and take a strong look at yourself in the mirror right now, and ask yourself, "Am I really and truly happy with my life? Am I fulfilled? Am I satisfied, or just comfortable? Do I feel complete? Have I served my life's mission, or is there more to my life, I am trying to avoid it? Why am I doing that? Am I really successful? Who am I?" If you said yes to all these questions, and you are sure that know who you are, stop reading. If you answered no to one or more of these questions and you are sure you do not know who you are, read on.

As women, we have mistakenly lived the lie of having to attend to the needs of others and to place ourselves dead last! No more. I declare and give you permission to *live life on your own terms Now!* It's ok to do so. Many of us have demonstrated great abilities to accomplish so much with only giving 60% of ourselves. How much more dangerous can we be if we give 100% of ourselves by being whole, fulfilled, and complete? I know there are parts of us that we hide, avoid, lock up, and keep. We pretend like these parts don't exist. We have learned through our upbringing, through society, and through other ways what is acceptable, what is unacceptable, what is rewarded, and what is punishable. We have learned how to put a mask on. We have learned to make our masks so convincing that others in our lives don't have a clue who we really are. Quite frankly, we don't have a clue of who we really are. We haven't given that other part of ourselves a chance to live or to shine, *until now*.

It is time for you to no longer suffer in silence. You can no longer accept the lie that you cannot live the life you really want to live. It is a choice. It is time to choose. I commend you on your choice today. Having possession of this book marks the day that you are deciding it's your turn now to live life on your own terms. Congratulations! I'm very happy for you, and look forward to helping you discover how to take your turn and live life on your own terms *right now.*

You may be saying, "That sounds great and all, but *how* can I live life on my own terms now?" I have that covered, so no worries. First, my hope and prayer for you as you read this book is that the following happen:

***You Live.*** Really live. Live in your fullness and in your totality. I hope that you start respecting and honor yourself by doing what makes you happy without feeling guilty, apologetic, or selfish.

**Be Free.** I hope that you realize you do not have to juggle all those balls in the air at the same time all the time. In fact, you can literally throw a couple of those balls away because you have juggled those same balls for a long time and you really don't have to anymore. I also hope you discover that you cannot be at two places at the same time, as hard as you may try to be. What I mean by that is, you cannot be a full time daughter to your parents when you are a full time mother and wife to your family. You will understand towards the end of the book.

**Be You.** Acknowledge, accept, and embrace you, the good, the bad, and the indifferent. As uncomfortable and as scary as that may seem, you will inevitably feel relieved that you chose to come from behind the masks, to become completely naked and real with yourself, and to accept your true authentic self. Listen, you may not know who you really are, and you may think it's too risky and costly for you and others to take the mask off. It's ok. It's time to live life on your terms, and doing so starts with being who you were born to be. Despite the challenges that come by *being you, taking this wonderful journey* will be the most rewarding experience of your life. Look at it this way: You have reached success as an incomplete, voided, emptied, broken, half of a self! Imagine how much more successful and powerful you will be once you get freed up to become your true, complete, fulfilled, whole, and imperfectly perfect self!

*It's your turn Now! Take it.*

# **Introduction**

Recently, I have asked myself many questions about happiness and success with regards to life and business, family and career, love and fulfilment. "What constitute success?" "What is success to me?" "What makes others successful *and others not successful?*" *"What is the one thing that is keeping me from being happy and successful right now?"*

Have you ever pondered any of these questions about yourself? What is holding you back from being happy and even more successful right now?

Mark Twain once said, *"The secret of getting ahead is getting started."* This is an absolute truth. No one has ever achieved anything without first making a start and an attempt. It is all about taking action, whether devising a plan, assessing all possible options, gathering your resources, and prepping for the journey. You have to get started in searching for your happy and your success. What is your happy? What constitutes success for you? And what is that one, or perhaps multiple things going

1

on in your world that is keeping you from being really and truly happy and even more successful in your life and business?

It's time for you to find out! It's your turn to get started on the journey of discovering yourself! It's your turn to make it all about you, and it's ok to do just that. It's your turn to do, live, and be happy while being successful. It's your turn to now to start living life *on your terms*!

# The Purpose of This Book

The purpose of this book is to motivate, inspire, and move you to think about what success means to you and how to pursue happiness. This book is intended to help you give yourself permission, without guilt or worry, to be *selfish*. It is time for you to have your turn NOW. It is your time to renew your shine, reclaim your time, and restore your life. You deserve it. Many successful people seem to be happy with their success, but it was with a cost that perhaps didn't need to be. It didn't need to be at your expense for the sake of others' successes, or for the sake of carrying the family tradition, or to prove to be someone in life to shut up the naysayers. This book guarantees to bring a different perspective and approach to living life on your own terms. It's Your Turn NOW gives frank, raw and powerful examples of Sarah's personal challenges and how she overcame them all by making it her turn NOW. Sarah provides case studies and excellent examples of other successful people who have recognized the secrets to living life on their own terms. She also provides step by step, simple and easy-to-use exercises on how to not only think about making it your turn to live life on your terms, but how to take action and sustain living life on your own terms. This book will help you discover how to truly be happy and successful all at the same time. It's Your Turn NOW!

# How to Use the Book

At the end of each chapter, there will be an exercise and reflection activity section. Please find a quiet space to read and complete the activities provided. All of the activities will help you reframe, refocus, and rethink on what happiness and success means to you.

After reading this book, please give yourself permission and take action into changing one thing you are doing, feeling, or thinking, and commit to making that change within a realistic and feasible time frame. Doing so will move you from taking action to sustaining and maintaining a happy and even more successful life and career.

In addition, please go to the resources page and view where to leave reviews and comments, as well as reviewing the different programs and services I offer by going to http://sarahreneelangley.com.

Remember, It's your turn *Now*! Take it! Enjoy the book. May it bless you and truly change your life.

# Chapter 1: IMPERFECTLY PERFECT

*"You are perfect for your imperfect situation...It all fits together nicely."*
**Dr. Sarah Renee Langley**

It is important to know that in life, no one is perfect. Let me repeat this again, "No one is perfect." Everything seen with the naked eye may appear to be perfect, be what you are really seeing are shades of imperfection glazed over to appear as perfection. It's all based on the perception and interpretation of where you, as the perceiver, are at the time of making an assumption.

When I was a young girl, I was nerdy in school. I was well-liked by my teachers, but hated and mistreated by some of my classmates. A teacher noticed that I couldn't sit still in my seat during class. He had noticed this for some time, as I would squirm and move so much in my chair. He sent me to the counselor's office for an anxiety assessment. Classmates found out about this and began teasing me. I felt so defective and unacceptable because of my hang-up. Interestingly, years later, I became a therapist with the ability to assess, diagnose, and treat anxiety symptoms through psychotherapy. Back then, I felt totally imperfect as I compared myself to others whom I thought were perfect because of their popularity, or because of their physical development that seemed perfect during that 7th grade puberty phase. Yet, I had discounted and ignored what teachers and family had praised me for. I was an intelligent, very ambitious, talented, and hardworking young lady. Consequently, I was willing to give that up in order to join the popular crowd of kids until my former 6th grade teacher, who loved me like a daughter and served as a second father-figure, set me straight. Mr. Parris, my beloved former teacher, reminded me of my inner strength, my resilience, and what my future held. He had me look past the current situation and reminded me of my upbringing, how I had people waiting on me to shine later in life, and encouraged me to stay focused on the course of my life. He even predicted I would end up driving around in my neighborhood in my Jaguar and see former classmates on the street hoboing and homeless! Well, it's a Mercedes that I now drive, but to see some former classmates on the streets or to find out they are no longer living, had me to wonder what was different about me. My classmates and I all grew up in the same neighborhood with, unfortunately, little to have in terms of money or resources. The difference was I had people in my corner telling me that I was *imperfectly perfect.*

I have a saying: *"There is no such thing as weaknesses, just uncultivated strengths waiting for a chance to grow."* It will take imperfect situations, coupled with our own quirkiness, hang-ups, and other idiosyncrasies to result in our imperfect perfection. Imperfectly perfect, to me, is the process of acknowledging, embracing, accepting, and honoring yourself in your entirety. Simply put, accept your good, your bad, and your ugly. Your imperfections are simply and wonderfully perfect. You have also been made perfect for your imperfect situations. And It all fits together nicely.

It's Your Turn NOW!

## Happiness and Success Story: Madame C.J. Walker

Have you ever heard of Madame C.J. Walker, an early 20th-century hair and beauty entrepreneur? Madame Walker is one of my heroes whom I love and respect to this day. Madame C. J. Walker, born Sarah Breedlove, was a producer of hair care products for African-American women and became very successful. In fact, she was one of the first American women to become a millionaire. Hearing this, you may think that Madame C.J. Walker was perfect and had the perfect life. On the contrary, Madame C.J. Walker and her life were anything but perfect. She chose to look beyond any imperfections she had and made the best use of her imperfect situation to transform her life.

Sarah, was orphaned at the tender age of six when her parents died from yellow fever. She was shuttled to her older sister's home in Vicksburg, Mississippi, and later began work as a housemaid. Like so many others, she soon found herself caught in the trap of little education and no opportunity to rise above and beyond, and so marriage seemed to be the most likely escape. She married Moses McWilliams at the young age of fourteen, and by age 18 had a daughter named Leila. After the death of her husband two years later, Sarah moved to St. Louis, Missouri and began the hard work of taking in laundry. She did this work for 18 years, as well as other domestic housework. Sarah's story does not end here; it's merely beginning.

As Sarah's imperfect situations persisted, she didn't let life or circumstances dictate her way of living. She made moves that resulted in her living the life she wanted on her own terms. In her late 30's, Sarah developed a formula for hair products as a result of her own experience with hair loss because of fatigue and the damaging products of her day. She often stated that the formula came to her after a time of prayer. Eventually, friends began to ask her for the formula, and Sarah soon began selling her own hair products to friends as well as door to door. Later, a move to Denver, Colorado in 1906 brought further success as she began to advertise her business with the help of her second husband, a newspaper man named Charles Joseph Walker. Sarah began to take his initials as her business name, Madame C.J. Walker, for which she is now known.

### It's Your Turn NOW!

The incredible story of how Madame C.J. Walker developed the hair care products which made her a millionaire is an example of a remarkable transformation. Slowly, her success story began with her attempts to improve her situation. It's interesting to note that Sarah's experimenting, or doing something new and different, resulted in her financial breakthrough. Walker's life had an eventful turnaround. On an interesting note, this success could have hit a standstill if Sarah had listened to her second husband. At the turning point in her career, he did not think her business could expand any further, but Sarah chose to listen to her inner voice instead. This division of opinion ended their marriage, yet Madame C.J. Walker continued to grow in her success. Not only did she create and market a variety of new hair care products for African Americans, but she also began to recruit "Walker Agents" to help sell her products, fought controversy over the hair care ideas of her time, and opened a school for "hair culturists." She travelled the world to recruit salespeople and demonstrate her products, and encouraged other African American entrepreneurs to go after their dreams.

By following her dream and listening to her inner voice, Madame C.J. Walker changed the face of history. The little girl orphaned at age 6, who grew up to be a laundry washer and housemaid had now become a millionaire success story. She indeed was imperfectly perfect.

Everyone wants to be successful, but not everyone wants to take the risk to try out something new and different that leads to both genuine happiness and success. You may ask yourself, "Who am I to do something new and different to be happy and successful?" Let's reframe this question to ask, "Who are you not to do this?" Walker didn't allow her circumstances nor her past to dictate her future. Walker went with her inner voice and passion and inevitably achieved success. Walker was imperfect, like all of us, yet her imperfect life was perfect for her. She was the right person for her predestined life. She fuelled her energies into rising above her situation and challenges. In other words, your life may have come with challenges that have resulted in mishaps, setbacks, and an overall sense of being stuck. However, you have pressed through the challenges because you were motivated to get to the top. Use your hang-ups, idiosyncrasies, or whatever else you deem unacceptable about yourself and let these all play part in your overall happiness success.

May I ask, what keeps you not wanting to embrace your imperfectly perfect self? Is it fear of failure? Did I hit a nerve? Let's explore this dirty word called failure, because oftentimes, successful women struggle with the fear to fail.

### Flaws

Despite the criticizing or absentee parent, the many times you failed while climbing your way to the top, the nasty divorce, the money problems, or whatever it was that motivated you to strive and survive, you did it! And all while being imperfect. Please give yourself credit for your perseverance, your pursuit, and your press. It is human nature to look at our flaws and our faults, but it is really our flaws and faults that make us imperfectly perfect. It makes us unique and different. Please do not hide or disconnect those parts which you deem as inappropriate and unacceptable. Who says those parts of you are inappropriate and unacceptable besides you? Perhaps you heard from others that it was unacceptable to be a certain way, or to look a certain way. Today, I want you to embrace that side of you that is deemed imperfect. I want you to give that part of you a chance to fully do, live, and be. Instead of thinking that by fully being you, flaws and all, will negatively impact your family, work, and success, why not reframe your thinking to embrace the notion that being fully you, flaws and all, will result in even greater success and an even greater benefit to everyone? And most importantly, making you really happy. Challenge your thinking about where those ideas come from, and consider why you feel or think that your imperfections are unacceptable. Do you think imperfections are not only flaws, but flaws that resulted from failures?

It's Your Turn NOW!
## What is Failure?

Amelia Earhart has been quoted as saying, *"Women must try to do things as men have tried. When they fail, their failure must be but a challenge to others."*

Amelia knew that what we think of as "failure" isn't truly failure. We are called to ponder on this statement, and to realize that everything carries a lesson. Amelia was telling us that even what we think of as failure carries a lesson that can be acted upon in further attempts at trying. Giving up is failure. I repeat, giving up is failure. Flaws are not results of failures, and failures are not results of flaws. Despite all of the odds in your pursuit of becoming happy and successful, do not give up. Giving up equates defeat. Notice that I did not say failure equates defeat.

First, failure is not when you have tried something and it didn't work out. Failure is quitting altogether. You may not have received that promotion you wanted and deserved, or your business venture may have fallen flat, but that's not failure. Failure is quitting and giving up. You have tried, and that is still success. As the expression goes, *"Nothing beats a what if than a try."* Unfortunately, we have processed defeat and losing as failure, and we internalize this idea as being one who is a loser and one who has failed. We often see failure as proof that success is unattainable, and that we are far from meeting our goals. In short, we take defeat personally, we feel like just giving up, and we cope by avoiding the emotions that result from failure and rejection. However, I come to tell you that it is a natural part of life and of our personal and professional growth. Use these moments as teachable moments. *Every day is not a good day, but every day is a learning day*!

History is full of people who didn't give up after multiple so called 'failures,' so you are in great company! Abraham Lincoln was demoted in the military, lost elections, and had many business failures. Oprah Winfrey was once fired from a job as a TV reporter because she was told that she was "unfit for TV!" A failed attempt is never a reason to not move forward. Imagine if these successful people had given up.

It's Your Turn NOW!

Studies have found that people who are optimistic about life and think they are healthy tend to live longer than people who think they are sick. Our minds have so much power if we use them for good, like with positive thinking. Our success in life has much more to do with how we view the world around us than we would think. People who think they have control over a situation will always be more successful than those who feel like everything just happens to them. When you have a setback, get rejected, or keep hearing no, it's time to take a step back and focus on what you can control. How can your failure give you valuable information for moving forward? What did it teach you to do or not do? Thinking of the setback as a set of facts rather than a reflection of your personality or self-worth will keep you from feeling overwhelmed and depressed about the experience.

## Fail Forward

People who *fail forward* also aren't afraid of rejection. So often the fear of hearing *no* keeps us from asking someone to give us a chance, or from asking for a deserved promotion, or even asking for help. If you can learn not to take rejection personally, then literally nothing will stop you from moving forward. You will be invincible. How do you learn to fail? The simple answer is that taking risks and asking for opportunities is a muscle you have to exercise every day. The great baseball player Babe Ruth is known for his many home runs, but he had twice as many strikeouts in his career. *"Every strike brings me closer to the next home run,"* he said. The great thing about getting used to hearing *no* is that eventually someone will say *yes*. So don't be afraid to fail, and embrace it as a part of life. Your successes will seem much sweeter after you've put in the effort to pick yourself up when you strike out.

### Happiness and Success Story: Arianna Huffington

Failure was not a choice for Arianna Huffington. During her growing up years, Arianna was taught by her mother that failure was not something to be afraid of. She learned that failure does not mean that success cannot be possible, but is a stepping stone toward success. This important lesson has been played out throughout her life. In her early teens she moved from Greece to England for college. Huffington has authored thirteen books since the 1970's, and is a well-known syndicated columnist. She had achieved much success in this area, and could have easily dwelled within her comfort zone of that success. But she decided to reach higher, and ran for Governor of California in 2003. Her campaign attempt failed, and she dropped from the race near the end of the election campaign. However, Huffington did not see this as a failure, but as a lesson to be learned. After reflecting upon her experiences, Huffington gained insight into the power of the internet, which was in its infancy at the time of her campaign. In 2005 she co-founded *The Huffington Post*, which is now a well-known news website. Huffington's success with this new venture was founded on the lessons from the failure of her election campaign; she was applying the notion of *failing forward*, as we previously discussed earlier in this chapter.

Therefore, take a deep introspection before you start your new journey, and don't expend too much time and energy trying to find out what you love doing the most. Deep down inside of your heart, you already know. It's just a matter of uncovering the dust to reveal the jewel. Know that you are a *Perfect Platinum, a Dynamo Diamond, a Precious Pearl.* All because you are *imperfectly perfect*.

**Give yourself this permission to be imperfectly perfect.**

# Exercise Activity: An Affirmation for Positivity

*Write 7 statements starting with "I Am . . ." Use positive and affirming statements of what you want to believe to be true about yourself. Then pick one statement that resonates most with you. Meditate on this, speak it aloud, and remind yourself throughout the day of this statement. Jot this here as your very first affirmation statement.*

_____

_____

_____

_____

_____

_____

_____

_____

_____

# Reflection Activity: What is Your Life Vision?

*Let the questions guide you in answering each question.*

What does your life currently look like?

_____

_____

_____

_____

What do you want your life to look like?

_____

_____

_____

_____

What prevents your life from being how you want it to look?

_____

_____

_____

_____

What is your passion? What makes your face light up?

_____

_____

_____

_____

## It's Your Turn NOW!

What do you find irritating? What causes you anger?

_____

_____

_____

_____

# Chapter 2: BE YOUR OWN BEST FRIEND

*"Reach way down, find your soul, take a look, take control, and really be who you are. Don't look back, find your start, and put your faith in the only one in whom you can depend. Be your own best friend, be your own best friend. Let your life begin. Be your own best friend."*
**Ray Stevens lyrics: Be Your Own Best Friend**

As previously mentioned, no one should be in control of your happiness or your success. Placing your happiness and success into someone else's hands can be equally likened to also putting your destiny and purpose into someone else's hands. I am not saying that you can't derive happiness and success from someone else, but don't ever let others tie you down to the extent that you are unable to fulfill your own purpose. Your significant other may be your best friend, and their intentions to ensure you aren't hurt or disappointed when going after what your want to do may be well and good. But please do not let anyone's opinions, perspectives, ideas, or suggestions, not even your loved ones, keep you from going after your dreams and pursuits. I have counseled many successful women who have buried their dreams and desires because their parents, friends, pastor, or husband said they needed to fulfil their husband's vision, or needed to first attend to the home and be a dutiful wife and mother. Many women I counseled confessed that they had witnessed their mothers give up on their dreams for the sake of the family. You may have heard or read somewhere that it is the woman's duty to ensure everyone else is taken care of, and that the woman's reward is seeing the success of everyone she helped to be successful. This is sad. You may not know your true inner passions because you have been so focused on fulfilling others' passions and pursuits. You are everyone's best friend, cheerleader, and confidant, and the one who pushes others to their happiness and success. Do you ever wish for someone to be and do the same for you? Why are you waiting for someone to be and do that for you? Can't you be your own best friend and push yourself to your own happiness and success, too?

You are a go-getter, ambitious, and hard driven. You know how to strive and excel in everything *that benefits others.*

Give yourself that same courtesy. You may say that you have benefited, too. *But have you?* Have you put any limits on yourself that withhold your capacity to do so much more? Has your significant other placed limitations on you to strive but so far and so much? Have you felt guilty to surpass your significant other and, therefore, play it small? Where have you seen that before? Why?

For Madame C.J. Walker, she did not let the love for her husband limit her in achieving her goals and ultimate success. She refused to be average, and in the process, her marriage suffered. I bring this up as a point. In your decisions of *living life on your own terms*, life as you know it will be impacted. And that's ok. You will move out of complacency and stagnation, which then changes the way you operate. Isn't it amazing how you may have thought you weren't stagnant because you have been successful and have had a good life? I am talking directly to your ability to *now live life on your own terms*. You know how to be successful and ambitious for the sake of others; it is time for you to be successful and ambitious for yourself, and only yourself as being the motivating factor. It is time for you to be your own best friend and strategize how you will discover your inner passions that have been buried for years, how you will identify self-sabotaging behaviors that kept you from being happier and successful, and how you will execute this new way of living, unapologetically and guiltlessly. Sometimes, people impose their hang ups on others to make themselves look great and others look bad. You may have a spouse or significant other who may not agree with something you want to do, and as a result, you question your priorities and your motives, and inevitably shelve your dreams. There's an anonymous quote that says, *"A man is only insecure about a female when he knows she deserves better."* You may have someone in your life who imposes their insecurities on you and makes you feel totally insecure, guilty, and too afraid to go after your dreams. With regard to Madame C.J. Walker, it would have been not only to her detriment if she had listened to her husband and not further advanced her career, but it would have been to the detriment of women who, to this day, are entrepreneurs in their own right because of Walker's desire to achieve greatness. I give you permission to stop being a *frienemy* to yourself, and to be your best friend *Now!* We can be such *frienemies* to ourselves instead of being such great BFFs with ourselves! Stop criticizing, judging, and comparing yourself to others. You are your own unique supreme, beautiful being, inside and out.

## Case Study: Me

When I was a little girl, I aspired to be a singer and fashion designer. My brothers said I could not sing, and that there was no money to be made in fashion designing. My parents wanted me to be a nurse, a teacher, or to marry a doctor. In my household I grew up with conflicting messages, having a critical father and a passive yet caring mother, as I attemtped to make them happy. My parents did not go to college and hoped that their children would finish school. Being the only daughter since my older sister passed away years before, the burden was on me to to lift up the family name. Today, I am a Doctor of Philosophy in Human Behavior, an owner of multiple businesses, and licensed in mulitple states as a Licensed

Professional Counselor, and I still felt like something was missing. I realized it was me, the little girl who wanted to be a singer and a fashion designer. I had buried her years ago, although she would come out from time to time, in my fashion sense, or in my singing in the shower. That part of me was always there, but it lay hidden because I was on a mission to make my family proud and raise up the family name by being one of the first on both sides of my family to hold a PhD. Everyone is happy and proud. But how about me? Yes, I have reaped the benefits of my hard work and efforts. But how much more satisfied, fulfilled, and happy would I have been if I had gone against my family's wishes, dealt with their disappointment, and had become a singer and fashion designer? Who is to say that this was my purpose and destiny? Truth be told, whatever your destiny or purpose is, I find that it will somehow be fulfilled, with or without your help or consent. Your life was mapped out before you arrived in this world, and all that has happened to you has played a part to get you to where you are today. I am speaking through firsthand experience that it is simply a matter of adding yourself into the equation and pursuing life on your own terms. Please do not wait until retirement age to pursue your dreams because the age limit seems to constantly and consistently change. You can manage your current obligations and still discover and pursue your inner passions. Even if your passion is totally different from what you know or currently do, it is *OK*. You will be happy that you chose to pursue your passion, after experiencing some initial shock, ambivalence, confusion, and sadness, of course!

Be your own best friend and live your life without caring about what other people think of you. Take your life to an even greater level by doing more of what you love. When it comes to what you love to do, there's an inner fire that cannot be quenched. No one can stop you from achieving your dreams if you are truly passionate about your dreams. Here's the thing, many do not know their true passion. Many are indecisive about their desires, and cannot determine if it is a true desire from within or if it is someone else's desire. Personally, I have lived this way.

### It's Your Turn NOW!

You no longer need to continue that old story of living for others any further. Yes, the story is familiar, it is comfortable, and it is easy to navigate through it. But why does this need to happen at your expense? This is not how life has to be for you. Life does not have to be at your expense all of the time. Make up in your mind to stop ignoring yourself. Stop ignoring that unction within, stop ignoring that inner quiet and still voice, stop ignoring that longing within your soul, and stop ignoring that deep knowing that's telling you that there's more to you than what you let on, and that you are to do something else. Frankly, you are more than what you do. What you do is not you, meaning, what role or position you hold does not identify or define who you really are. You may not clearly know who you really are or what your purpose is, but the only way to discover this is to first acknowledge there is something tugging at you from within, and it is time to accept this and address it. *Right now.*

It is totally understandable that as a child you may have seen your mother, grandmother, aunt, older sister. or cousin dress up in their work uniform, or head to the office, and perhaps you said to yourself, *"When I grow up, I am going to be just like her."* You may have become the same professional as your mom, grandmother, aunt, older sister, or cousin. Perhaps you realized later, however, that you didn't necessarily like that profession. You could easily do it and be totally successful in it, but you are bored with it. You may feel unfulfilled or empty inside despite the success. You may have inadvertently discovered that you love to cook and desire to be a caterer and own a catering business. Perhaps you get excited when asked to cook or make a delicious dish. Consequently, in college, you pursued the major that resulted in landing a job like your mom, grandmother, aunt, older sister, or cousin. Perhaps you currently are in that same job and these ladies in your life are happy for you. Sadly, you may not be happy for *you*. You may go to the office with a smile on the outside, but silently, you are screaming on the inside. You chose to live the lifestyle of someone else because of the reward of praise, recognition, and acceptance. You justify the benefits of working that job or

32

profession by the substantial amounts of money you make. You have seen how it made the ladies in your life happy. Or did it really? How do you know if they were really and truly happy? Your mom, grandmother, aunt, older sister, and cousin may have done the same thing you have done, which is living for someone else's approval. You did not pay attention to the beam in your eyes regarding cooking because you heard or assumed that there wasn't a career or money to be made in catering. Money doesn't result in consistent happiness. Being true to who you are by doing what you love, while making money in doing it, results in consistent happiness.

### Steps to Happiness and Success

Now, happiness is relative. You have to first identify what lights you up and pay close attention to it. If you need to journal or write down every time you light up and get happy, write it down before you forget! Next, define what happiness and success are for you. That will point you in the right direction in exposing yourself to your inner passion and finally begin an introduction, or really, a reaquaintance with the other side of you. It is time for you to *Live Now*! *Full, whole, and complete.* Otherwise, unhappiness and unfulfillment will be your reward for not taking action in pursuing your passions. Just being honest.

Be your own best friend, not your own *frienemy*. Take off the limits. It's ok to go after that dream or desire that you may have put on the backburner. Do whatever you are passionate about and keep doing it; be more passionate about it, and ensure that you are happy in doing so. And most importantly, please love yourself to life! Address the areas which make you feel unloved or that keep you from fully loving and accepting all of yourself. Be your own best friend, accept yourself entirely, and live your life to the fullest. That is the correct order. Stop pouring yourself onto everyone when you are on E and pulling on reserves that were depleted years ago. Replenish yourself beyond going to the spa or doing yoga. It is time for you to stop and breathe, exhale, reflect, assess, accept, analyze, acknowledge, embrace, and love all of you, in mind, in body, and in spirit. Life is very short, and you have the opportunity and the choice to love yourself, pursue your passion, and fulfil your unique purpose on Earth. I pray for you to be full and fulfilled, and as Iyanla Vanzant says, to be in peace, not in pieces.


*Remember, accept and embrace you first. It's time to be your own best friend.*

# Exercise Activity: An Affirmation of Gratitude

*What are you grateful for in your life and/or your relationships? List 10 things please. Refer to this daily and recite to yourself before starting your day and before going to bed.*

_____

_____

_____

_____

_____

_____

_____

_____

_____

_____

_____

_____

# Reflection Activity: *Setting Your Goals*

*Find a quiet space to reflect on these questions before moving to the next chapter.* Take some time to consider your plan and the steps you will take for achieving each of your goals. *Please write your answers here.*

Write down what you would love to achieve within 5 years for your life. Set these goals as your short term and secondary goals.

_____
_____
_____
_____

Additionally, write down what you would love to have accomplished within the next 10 years, and set these as your long term and primary goals.

_____
_____
_____
_____

Please make sure that your goals are feasible and realistic to implement and achieve. In fact, you can make your goals SMART or SIMPLE.  We will discuss this process a bit later in the book.

# Chapter 3:  YOU ARE ENOUGH

*"Aerodynamically, the bumblebee shouldn't be able to fly, but the bumblebee doesn't know this so it flies anyway."*
**Mary Kay Ash**

As you read this book, it will seem like I need therapy! I assure you, I am ok, I have had plenty of therapy sessions in my time, and *I* was once a clinical therapist! At one point I realized, with the help of my therapist, that I felt defective. That was my dreaded place. We discovered that my feeling defective linked back to my relationship with my father. I did not feel like I was enough to him. My therapist helped me trace my daddy issues back to my relationships with guys and my apparent mistrust of them. She also identified my masculine energy as it played in my ambition, academic pursuits, and career choices throughout my life. I was trapped in a state of wanting to prove that I was enough. I was often perplexed at how my relationships turned out. Looking back, I was the 'man' in the relationship and often attracted to men who were passive, easy going, and peaceable. They were in fact, the 'women' in the relationship! I knew I brought much to the table to be desired, yet, it still didn't seem enough nor acknowledged. I lived this never ending cycle pursuing men who were just like my *DADDY*! Although I was a therapist, I couldn't really see this problem until another therapist illuminated it for me. Initially, this triggered insecurities and self-criticism for the fact that I couldn't identify my own hang-ups. It was depressing to say the least. But afterwards, it was refreshing to pinpoint the problem and 'fix it'.

What are your cycles and patterns? Where do you feel like you are just not enough? What are the triggers that come up for you? Pay attention to how you operate around certain people versus others in your life. In the meantime, constantly tell yourself, "I am enough." No matter the situation or where you are in your life, let this be your mantra. Refuse to be intimidated and refuse to play small because others in your environment choose to do so. If you are in an environment where you are the smartest person and others in your environment play small, it's time to move! Get out of that environment and either go to a new one or create a new one and surround yourself with those who are smarter, better, and more advanced than you so that you can glean from them. Stop pretending to be the chicken that doesn't fly just to fit in with the others in your circle, and be the eagle that you were born to be and soar with other eagles! Create a different environment that waters, nurtures, embraces, and accepts your total uniqueness and greatness. You know how to do all of these for others, and I am encouraging you to do it for yourself *Now*.

Please note that your happiness is not contingent upon *who* you are or *what* you have. Your happiness is predicated by *what* you think. I repeat, your happiness is predicated by what you think. The way you think determines how you behave. When you wanted to be financially well-off, you had to first believe it as true for you and then you inevitably became financially well-off. It is not a matter of seeing to believe. Rather, its converse is a more truer statement. You have to believe it to see it. You have to be laser focused on your happiness and your success to obtain both. I am preaching to the choir, I know! You have already proven this to be fact when you became focused based on whatever motivating factor propelled you to become wealthy, successful, and accomplished in your life. So why not be laser focused now and aceept that you are enough? You were more than enough when you achieved your wealth and your success. You were more than enough when you took care of all of your obligations and responsibilities. You had enough confidence, wisdom, courage, and gusto to make things happen. So why not be your own motivating factor, recognize that you are enough, and go after your happinesss and your success? It is Ok to do so. I give you permission to make yourself the motivating factor to pursue your passion and purpose for your own sake, and not for the sake of others. Again, you know how to be successful for the sake of your kids' education and their well-being, for your business partner's success, and also for the sake of your team's elevation and opporutinity for success. What about just doing it for *you* and you alone? It doesn't make you a bad person if you decide to live life for *you* on your own terms *Now*. You were enough to get the job done for everyone's benefit. Now, apply that same way of thinking towards your happiness and success for yourself, and look forward to the benefits of that excellent decision. This is merely a way to re-channel your time, energy, and money toward the right path for you. Despite any potential ups and downs or struggles, do not limit yourself any further. You are enough, and you can be happy and successful. It is time for you to step out and be the true and living *You* that you were born to be, *Right Now!*

### Happiness and Success Story: J.K. Rowling

Ralph Waldo Emerson said, *"To be yourself in a world that is constantly trying to make you something else is the greatest achievement."* To be successful in a world that tries to limit your potential and keeps you locked in antiquated roles by declaring them as your identity is definitely challenging. Society, modeled behavior, our upbringing, and whatever else that's included in the mix, further exacerbate our role and identity confusion. Here is your opportunity *today* to come to know who you are and proclaim that you are *enough*. You are beyond any role or position that you may hold. Your essence is

42

not defined by these roles. You make up the role and position with your uniqueness and beautiful personality. Your name is *NOT* Mom, Wife, Boss Lady, Manager, Employee, or Girlfriend. Your name is (insert your name here), a great, successful, beautiful, and wonderful woman who *is* a Mom, Wife, Boss Lady, Manager, Employee, or Girlfriend. Please no longer rob the world of who you truly are. We know what you bring to the table. *You need to Know it and Own it,* just like J.K. Rowling did.

Most successful and powerful women in the world tend to have their own rags to riches story. The story of Joanne Kathleen Rowling, the famous author of the Harry Potter series of books, is quite inspiring. J.K. Rowling, as she is widely known, had a difficult life, much as Madame C.J. Walker did. She was born in England in 1965, and began writing at the very young age of 6. She has often said that she grew up wanting to be a writer, but life got in the way, as it sometimes does, and her writing succumbed to her daily responsibilities. While traveling by train in 1990, Rowling's mind flashed with the beginning ideas for what would become the famous Harry Potter series. Consequently, it would be 7 long years before this idea would come to fruition. Rowling recalls that year as one of difficulty. The first setback was the loss of her mother. Then, she travelled to Portugal, having taken a position to teach English as a means of coping with her enormous grief and also as a way of financially supporting herself. Two years afterward, Rowling married a Portuguese television journalist. This was, however, a brief marriage and they soon separated. Rowling travelled across the ocean, returning to England with her daughter, Jessica. Those were, perhaps, her most difficult days as she struggled as a new and single mother. She often battled poverty and depression as she tried to provide for her daughter on a very limited income through public assistance. She often wrote in cafes while her daughter napped, and has said that she "was as poor as it is possible to be." However, she recognized that she was enough by knowing that her purpose was to write.

Rowling's happiness and ultimate success was rooted in her love for writing. She motivated herself by doing what she loved most. Rowling knew that sulking and sobbing would not make her problems go away, and she refused to give in to misery. Instead, she made plans to move forward and do something different contrary to her situation. She mixed passion, purpose, and action together to produce a wonderful result that benefited many, but only *after* it first benefited her. Today, the world knows her for the wildly-successful Harry Potter book series and the movies developed from them.

J.K. Rowling is one of the most renowned successful women in the world, and this is due to the fact that she decided she was *enough*. She realized she was enough to turn her misfortune into a fortune. Rowling realized she was enough to live out her passions despite the odds. She realized, embraced, and accepted that she was enough to dare to dream and take action to follow her passions and dreams. Although it may have been hard, and no matter the motivating factor that propelled her to write, she kept going and never gave up. Her manuscripts were reject three times; she could have easily said to herself, "*I am not* good enough after all." But Rowling did not allow the negative thinking to derail, detract, or distract her in her continual movement. She believed first and then she saw it, and at last she received the bountiful benefits.

## Steps to Passion and Purpose

I want to reiterate the order in which you should commence the pursuit of your passion and purpose. First, make it about you and be your own motivating factor, instead of using factors that are do or die and having you think you must accomplish your goals. "I must," "I need," or "I have to," for the sake of your family, kids, the family name, or your livelihood, are nerve wracking, anxiety provoking, and stressful. This way of thinking inevitably thwarts and paralyzes you to the point of burnt out. Coincidentally, you already know that way of doing things, now let's do something differently, shall we?

Next, show the same courtesy to yourself the way you show it to everyone else. Make yourself your first priority. From there, others will reap the benefits. Societally, we tend to reward sacrifice more than we tend to reward excellence. Have you noticed this? A person could be giving up their home, car, food, marriage, or all of their money for the pursuit of accomplishing a significant goal that's considered to be recognized. Yet we don't seem to reward a person who instead has consistently done everything in excellence without having to sacrifice their basic needs.

## Case Study: Me

When I was younger, I was a very ambitious child, and a hardworking A and B student. I was praised in school for my efforts, but not necessarily praised at home because it was always expected as the norm for me to do well. When my brothers brought in D's and F's, but worked hard to get C's by sacrificing extracurricular activities, they were recognized for their efforts by bringing better grades. When I did not do well in something, negative attention, disappointment, and constant reminders of the time I wasn't 'so perfect' resulted. I felt like I was not enough and even unimportant at times. Consequently, in my years of counseling children and families, I have found that most children who do exceptionally well in school, but lack the attention and praise for their accomplishments, tend to feel neglected and overlooked. Oftentimes, these children hide their problems, and sadly, their problems go unnoticed. Many of them perceive that something is wrong with them, and as a result, their unresolved problems significantly impact their mental, emotional, and at times, their physical states. Regrettably, these children believe they are not enough. Many of them try to overcompensate for their perceived lack within themselves, and become overdriven to do above and beyond the call of duty in their lives and in their careers as adults. This is where stress and burnout happens. Moreover, this type of thinking and behavior spills over into adulthood and is frequently relived all over again through their own children, *Until Now*. It stops here. I declare that *You Are Enough.*

*YOU ARE ENOUGH.* You no longer need to continue that old cycle. Nor do you have to prove or vie for affection and attention. At times, people look for affection and attention in unlikely places, as the song goes "Looking for love in all the wrong places." When love and affection are not at home, love and affection are sought after at work, by friends, or consequently, in affairs, in midnight snacks, in drinking, or in shopping. Honestly, I have sought affection and attention elsewhere. At one point, I looked for a nurturing family within my staff, until my therapist called me out on that, too, and stated that I needed to have more structure and boundaries. I was trying to fill a void that I had masked through my being ambitious and hard-driven. However, this only continued the vicious cycle of feeling defective and feeling like I was not enough. We tend to subconsciously seek after people who reminds us of those we had problems with from our previous personal or professional relationships, in hopes to bring closure and resolution to unresolved issues a second time around. Unfortunately, trying to resolve matters this way only further exacerbates the problem and continues the lie that we are not enough.

I say to you, make yourself first. Pursue your passion and purpose for your sake. That is the correct order. Reframe your mindset, and believe and accept that your obligations will not be negatively impacted. Reframe your mindset and believe and accept that your obligations will, in fact, significantly benefit

49

from you putting yourself first. Know your true worth. Know your significance. Be true to yourself. Respect your boundaries. In fact, pay attention and listen to your inner self, and honor your boundaries. Come to know yourself. Declare *You Are Enough.* You no longer need to be stuck. *You Are Enough.* It *Is Not* too late. *You Are Enough.* Regardless of what others say, *You Are Enough.* Regardless of your past, *You are Enough.* Even if you 'failed' the first one million times, *You Are Enough.* Regardless of having previously placed your true desires on the backburner, or that you don't know which way to go next, *You, my friend, Are Enough.* As they tell us on the airplane, put your oxygen mask on first so that you can be fully alert in helping others put on their oxygen masks. We must help ourselves first in order to effectively and accurately help others. While at first I thought it as selfish to put my oxygen mask on first, I get it now. I hope you do, too.

**Remember, *you are enough.***

# Exercise Activity:  An Affirmation of being Enough

*Please write 15 ways that you are enough, and then recite each one this first thing in the morning, before going to work, during work, after work, before dinner, AND before going to bed:*

*Feel free to add additional affirmations of being enough here, and include in your daily reciting ritual for at least 30 days.*

_____

_____

_____

_____

_____

_____

_____

_____

_____

_____

_____

_____

_____

_____

_____

_____

_____

# Reflection Activity: Test and Prove the Naysayers

*Find a quiet space to reflect on these questions before moving to the next chapter. Write your answers here. The goal is to start developing the habit to reframe your thinking by saying differently to yourself what has been said about your so as to build up your esteem through self-validation.*

*Step 1. Make a list of up to 10 things that others say about you.*

_____

_____

_____

_____

_____

_____

_____

_____

_____

_____

_____

_____

_____

_____

_____

# It's Your Turn NOW!

*Step 2. Make a list of up to 10 perceptions you have of yourself, whether good or bad.*

_____

_____

_____

_____

_____

_____

_____

_____

_____

_____

_____

_____

_____

_____

_____

*Step 3. Next, make a list of 10 validation points that counter what you wrote in the list of statements and perceptions.*

_____

_____

_____

_____

_____

_____

_____

_____

_____

_____

_____

_____

_____

_____

# Meditation Pause

*You are approaching midway into the book.
Congratulations on your press and continued reading!
I am sure I have stirred all kinds of emotions, thoughts,
and feelings, and that's great! I want to take a pause,
kind of like an intermission during a theatre play, and
regroup ourselves and prepare for the next remaining
chapters. By the way, thank you, and I am very proud
of you.*

*I would like for you at this time, to give yourself the
courtesy in creating reflection time in a quiet space,
preferably with no one around, and sit relaxed and
upright, feet planted on the floor, and close your eyes.
Take 3 deep breaths, in and out, and pay attention to
any and everything that comes up. Do this for about
10 minutes.*

*Write down any thoughts, feelings, and emotions that came up.*

_____
_____
_____
_____
_____
_____
_____
_____
_____
_____

# It's Your Turn NOW!

*I ask that you repeat this exercise at your leisure for 1 week. Look back at all that you have written down so you can connect the dots. Analyze any words, paragraphs, and sentences that are similar or repeat themselves. Write them here.*

_____

_____

_____

_____

_____

_____

_____

_____

*Then create 3 columns for sorting out these words and phrases. The First column will be for words that are repeated. The second column is the "How You Feel" column. Notice your feelings and thoughts in connection to the first column of words and phrases. The third column is the "Unrepeated or Confused" column. Here you will note any words, sentences or phrases that were not repeated, yet stood out.*

| Repeated Words | How I Feel | Unrepeated Words |
|---|---|---|
|  |  |  |
|  |  |  |
|  |  |  |
|  |  |  |
|  |  |  |
|  |  |  |
|  |  |  |
|  |  |  |
|  |  |  |
|  |  |  |
|  |  |  |
|  |  |  |

*This exercise will help you become aware of your inner thoughts and feelings, as well as give a sense of direction on where to begin in your journey towards happiness and greater success. You will know what to do once you do this. Know that you can do this. You can be happy and more successful and all just for you. Do not be scared. Do not worry. Do not fret. Do not fear.*

*It is time to <u>Stop Existing and Start Living.</u>*
*<u>It's Your Turn Now.</u>*

# Chapter 4: IT'S NOT OUT THERE IT'S IN THERE

*"The answers you seek are not without, they are always within, and have been there all the time waiting for you to discover them right at the nick of time."*
**Dr. Sarah Renee Langley**

The answer to true happiness and riches lies within you. Have you ever heard this phrase? Do you believe this statement? The answers to your problems are really deep inside of you. Yet a war within you surges because it is a war between your desires and your reality. What is the ideal thing to do, and what is the realistic choice? The war is being fought between the differing voices of your heart and mind. Your mind is there to serve and protect you, and as a result, your mind keeps you trapped inside a box. Ironically, the instructions on how to escape out of the box lies outside of the box! How do you get the instructions then? Let's take a step back and recall our earlier discussion about how we often stuff away and bury the deeper longings within our hearts. These longings need to be answered. They may lie buried for many, many years but, in the end, we will suffer if they remain unexpressed and buried. To be fair, your mind has served its purpose, but it's also keeping you incomplete by having you play it safe and keep your passions buried. How much more could you accomplish if you just listen to your inner self? There will always be a battle between your mind and your heart until that which is fed the most wins. The more you focus on fear, then the more you will play safe and, quite honestly, stay incomplete and insignificant. The more you reframe your focus on your happiness and success, then the more you will take action to move toward fulfilling your purpose and actualizing your dreams. Take this first step towards your happiness and success so that you are one step closer to the next step. Do not predetermine the results. You do not know how it will play itself out until you take action towards your happiness and success. Your process is no different than the processes you went through to become successful It is no different than what you have done to be in a position to provide for your family so well. Apply your process to this pursuit of true happiness and success for yourself *Now*.

It's Your Turn NOW!

## Happiness and Success Story: Sheila Marcelo

Similar to the lives of Madame C.J. Walker and J.K. Rowling, Sheila Marcelo's story is quite inspiring. Sheila Marcelo grew up in the Philippines, and often followed her parents around the rice mill that they ran. While there, she seemed intrigued by the workers, and often peppered them with questions about their work. Little did she know, but she was following her natural curiosity for technology and entrepreneurship. But in her family, as in many, each of the children were on a path toward a specific career. Her path was designated as a lawyer. Sheila applied and was accepted to Harvard Law School. Having taken several positions in the area of litigation, she decided to defer her entrance and instead apply to Harvard Business School. Sheila was beginning to listen to her deepest inner voice, rather than take the predetermined path that had been set for her by her family. It would have been easy for her to ignore that inner voice, particularly since at the time she was a new wife and mother and had many responsibilities.

It was during this time that Sheila held top managerial positions with several start-up companies, one of which was structured to help families raise money for college planning. Building on her love for technology and entrepreneurship, Sheila also was drawn to begin a company that would fill a need for families. As a young mother, she found herself in a position of seeking care for her children and also for her aging parents. She knew that her situation was not unique, and it fueled the development of her own business called Care.com. Today, it is the world's largest online resource for finding family care, and has 18 million members in more than 16 countries, with me personally, having been a member and having utilized their services before.

Sheila could have ignored her inner voice, and walked down the predetermined path that had already been laid about by her family. This would have been particularly easy given her responsibilities as a wife and mother. But it was these very responsibilities that also fueled her heart toward her predestined path. She chose to obey that call, and as a result, she ended up being even more successful. I am personally glad she obeyed that call, as Care.com blessed me with wonderful services for my mother. Thank you Sheila. You never know that which you are called can impact others you have never, or will never meet.

Women like Madame C.J. Walker, J.K. Rowling, Sheila Marcelo, and countless others not only were successful in what they have done, but their products and services have impacted many lives which has only added to their successes. These women knew what they wanted, realized their skills, and leveraged their efforts to grow and capitalize in their businesses. They committed to giving their all to realize their gifts and talents with excellence. They were able to recognize that the key to their happiness and success was right inside of them. *It is all about listening to your inner self and knowing that it is not really out there, it is really in there.*

## Case Study: Me

When I was younger, I felt that I had so much to prove. I was a little bit; in other words, I was skinny, nerdy, and picked on often. I grew up in a home where my brothers and I were often criticized for making mistakes. *"There is no room for mistakes,"* my father always said to us. All the contradicting and confusing messages supplemented my war within myself, to the point that I still have a private war or two to this day. Unfortunately, warring within myself also cluttered the answers within me. I have been so indecisive and fearful of making wrong decisions in my life that I did make huge mistakes that were almost detrimental to my future family. A great battle was forged in my mind! I played it safe, at times, unwilling to take risks to refrain from the possibility of embarrassment and ridicule. Yet, there was such a great longing to do more. So much more. But I didn't know what *more* was. Many could see more in me, but I couldn't. Then, one day, life happened.

I lost my job! I lost plenty of jobs many times over! Talk about being wide open and transparent, wow! I hope I am setting examples for you to do the same so that you can practice setting your own self free! I can't believe I am admitting this, but yes, I could not work for anyone. Either I was laid off, or fired. I couldn't see it then, but I was quite cocky, condescending, and controlling. I justified my actions, such as coming in late because I was caring for my ailing parent, or because the distance was long in travel, or accidents on the road prevented me from getting in on time, etc. etc. etc. I would stay late for work to make up the time. But apparently that was not enough to some managers. So the last time I was fired, I realized that I simply had to work for myself. Talk about a war within myself! I was quite fearful of being out on the street. But even worse was the dreaded fear that my dad and brothers would find out that I had 'failed' and that I would be forced to return home to live with my parents! For me, these dreaded fears outweighed the fear of starting my own business. So I started my counseling business in the basement of my home and then grew it from there. I did it. *Scared. Fearful. Afraid. But I did it*, scared, fearful, and afraid. I had to quench the war within myself by going deeper within myself. I went past my feelings and emotions to find the hidden meaning of my existence. I knew there was more to life than that for me, even though I did not know what that was just yet. I had to go past my hang-ups within me because my future depended on it. This led to an increase of self-reflection, therapy, and more praying. Thinking back to my humble beginnings with starting my own business, it was necessary for me to clean up my act for the sake of maintaining and sustaining my new business. I had to give myself the courtesy of establishing rules and boundaries in order to build a great name for myself. That meant no more being late, cocky, condescending, or controlling. RESET, LLC was officially born, and now I had to nurture and grow my new baby!

I have shared my story to illustrate to you that *The Answer* for your happiness and success *Is Not Out There, It's In There*. My answer for financial success wasn't necessarily in working for someone else. It was in working for me. I would not have known that had life not happened. My hang-ups, coupled with inevitability and with my destiny, brought about my very first clinical private practice called Restoring Every Soul Each Time, LLC also known as RESET, LLC. I remember watching the singer Beyoncé on an awards show and I was just hating on her! My then boyfriend at the time saw me fuming and questioned why. I was wondering how someone could just sing and dance and get paid millions of dollars for entertaining others while I worked daily saving lives from committing suicide, having nervous breakdowns, or murdering people, and barely got paid. Then it hit me! Do what she did! So I did. I realized that I was hating on her because she seemed to be living her dream and living her life. She was doing something fun and what she loves to do, and she gets enormously paid for doing something fun and what she loves to do. Whereas, I was stressed out, maxed out, and burnt out helping others get stable and re-established with their grip on reality. Doing my counseling business on a day to day basis only afforded my getting paid a minimum of $5 dollar co-pays by clients and then waiting months for the medical insurance companies to pay the remaining $45 dollars. It was safe and secure, in my mind at least, to let the insurance companies pay me, promote me, and send me clients. The war within me came down to the fact that I knew there was so much more for me to do beyond the therapy sessions. Yet I was afraid of not knowing what it looked like outside of what I knew. I was too afraid to step outside of my comfort zone.

It wasn't until I could no longer keep my business, staff, offices, and licenses that my mind began to change. I could no longer afford my counseling business. Life happened again, and I had to start from scratch. Except this time, I started over better, much more wisely, and correctly. I decided that I would do what I love to do in the process. Although I loved counseling, I desired to do what I love on a greater scale. It was through attending my favorite conference, New Peaks Millionaire Mind Intensive (now called Millionaire Mind Experience), that I discovered my passion to speak, teach, and coach to larger crowds, as well as writing, mentoring, training, and masterminding. I discovered that I can make a significant impact to others by taking my skills and knowledge base to greater heights and depths. Everything I have learned is founded on my long-held belief that every single thing happens for a reason. But I first had to push through my fear and win the war within myself. I had to embrace the fact that there would be challenges along the way, and accept that it was necessary to shift my focus on the benefits and rewards rather than on the challenges and obstacles. I came to the reality that the answer was not out there, it was truly in there. And in doing so, I have found greater success, true happiness, and started to become very acquainted with the other part of me I buried a very long time ago.

## Steps to Knowing What's in There

The answer is within you. But in order to discover what lies within, you must dig deep by spending time in self-reflection, and then go past your feelings, emotions, fears and doubts. Do not discount, discredit, or dismiss anything that comes up because you are tapping into your subconscious and this is truly where the answers lie. Actually, the subconscious mind is really the driving force to our decisions, actions, and emotions. Stop predetermining things by questioning how you will make this, that, or the other happen. You need to simply take that first step, which is to search within, and then write down everything that comes up for you and then prepare to take action. In the long run, you will be glad that you took action to discover the answers within yourself.

Know that it is not too late to discover the answers within yourself. You are not behind in the race, even if you think you are. Trust me, everyone will be amazed and jealous at how happy and successful you are all because you took the time to discover the answers within yourself on how to live your life. It is time to be happy and successful. Please do not try to convince yourself that you are happy, however, while feeling empty and missing inside. Being happy and empty inside can not coexist together. Do not deceive yourself with this lie. That is being comfortable, not happy and successful. No longer make being comfortable your truth and playing small your reality. All that you need to be happy and successful have been with you all this time. Now, if you like being comfortable and are satisfied with your life as is, then so be it. Accept that and move on. Just do not complain that something is missing and that you feel empty inside. It must be one or the other; either pursue your true happiness and success, or remain where you are in your life and

be happy about that. Again, both cannot exist.

*Remember, it's not out there, it's in there.*

# Exercise Activity: An Affirmation for ME

*Read this statement aloud with a strong and confident voice. You may repeat it as many times as you would like, and you may look in the mirror when you say these words. Then, think of at least 3 things about you that are unique. Write these down here and add to these affirmations.*

Today, I am connected firmly and passionately to my true self!

Today, I realize my potential, and I honor it by allowing myself to be uniquely me!

What's Unique about me are the following:

_____

_____

_____

_____

_____

_____

_____

# Reflection Activity: Respect Your Slots

*I would like for you to look at your calendar that you have filled with so many appointments and responsibilities. Are you scheduled in your calendar? Put yourself down. In fact, I want you to rearrange your calendar by listing half hour blocks, from the time you get up to the time you go to bed, from Sunday through Saturday. Fill in all that you do throughout your week. You may notice some of the slots are unfilled. See, you do have a moment for yourself! Perfect, pen yourself into that time and do not bump yourself off by putting another appointment or errand in that time slot.*

*From there, add times of meditation and reflection for yourself to refresh, regroup, and refocus for your day. Do this for 14 days and write here what thoughts, feelings, and emotions came up in doing this. Please continue to do this activity so you know how to respect your slots.*

_____

_____

_____

_____

_____

_____

_____

_____

_____

# Chapter 5: GIVE YOURSELF PERMISSION

*"When you give yourself permission to communicate what matters to you in every situation you will have peace despite rejection or disapproval. Putting a voice to your soul helps you to let go of the negative energy of fear and regret."*
**Susan L. Adler**

The wear and tear of fear and stress have an impact on our emotional, mental, and psychical health. Seeking approval from others, the need to prove yourself, or keeping on the mask, are all not worth your life. Reframe your mindset to focus on the higher goal of happiness and success. Focus only on that goal, and embrace all that comes with completing that goal so that there are no surprises and you have planned accordingly. As a matter of fact, I challenge you to start exposing yourself to something different and extraordinary just for yourself! Have you ever had a passion for art, music, photography, or sky diving? Why not schedule something totally different and out of the norm for you? What I want you to do is this: *Give Yourself Permission.* Your mind may say you don't have time for

72

yourself. I will start the trend and set the example here by telling you to tell your mind shut up and thanks for sharing. Then tell your mind that you are giving yourself permission to do whatever it is that you want to do. *It's Your Turn Now.*

I love traveling. I love going to distant places and learning about the culture and history of the towns, cities, and countries. My stinking thinking mindset, in its attempt to protect me, usually tells me that I don't have the money or the time to travel. But when I shift my focus on doing what I love to do, I am afforded the opportunity to travel at least 20 weeks throughout the year. I meet new people all the time and learn so much on my travels. I give myself permission to do what I love.

Give yourself permission to start something daring yet small that will put you in the groove to then doing something even more daring and much bigger. Step out of your comfort zone. Give yourself permission to pursue your happiness and success by working on exit strategies from your old ways, old habits, and old patterns. Give yourself permission to make room for the new, whether that means quitting your job, firing yourself from your business, getting a divorce, kicking out your 30-year-old kids, or putting your mother-in-law into the nursing home. There! How does that feel for you? I merely stated what you were thinking. Give yourself permission to think and say, and to even do what is *Best for You.* That is the point that I am making. What is best for you? We have been trained since forever to think about everyone else, and that our rewards for our sacrifices are in Heaven. Or at least at retirement age. NO! Surprisingly, what is best for you is also what's best for the entire situation and for everyone involved.

## Violating Your Boundaries

Imagine a football field with a line cut straight down the middle, splitting the two sides evenly from the 50-yard line. You are on one end, and everyone else in your life is on the other end. Your role and position is to tend from your goal line to the 50-yard line. This means that the area from the goal line to the 50-yard line is your responsibility. Everyone else in your circle has the responsibility to tend to the space from the 50-yard line to their goal line. But, here is the problem that I have often found with clients, especially couples; you not only handle your responsibilities between your goal and the 50 yard line, but often cross over the 50-yard line to attend to everyone else's responsibilities on their end. Why? Is it because you think that you can do it better, faster, easier, or accurately? Here's the clincher; you are upset because your same circle of people is not lifting a finger to assist you, and that they do not do their part altogether because they expect you to do it all. Would you like to know the reason why they are not lifting a finger to assist you and why they aren't doing their part and expecting you to do it? Here's why: *You are doing it.* Period. There's no need for them to do their job because you are doing yours and theirs, too! They will perhaps only do 10% of what's left or permitted. You usually take care of the 90%! What's left to do? You cannot expect your circle to respect your boundaries and structure if you don't *respect your boundaries and structure yourself.*

Here's another way of looking at it. You are the nucleus or keystone of your circle. You nurture and attend to the needs of everyone surrounding you, but you may expect the same courtesy extended to you. Why do you expect that? You and your circle created the script for everyone! You are the director of this movie! Your responses, actions, and reactions will dictate how everyone else responds, acts, and reacts. Their job is to take. Your job is to give. The end. It is not in their job description to give, otherwise it throws off the direction of the dynamic that has been set in place. In other words, the only way that you will get anything from this equation is to give yourself permission to create a new circle in a new environment. I am not necessarily saying divorce your family or quit your job (yet), but I am suggesting that you create your very own environment that has everything that you want and need. Do you know what you want and need? That is where you start. Write down what you want and need in this new environment so that you can escape to, dwell in, and operate in to be fully replenished, and to then go back and give of yourself to your circle in your current environment. Please give yourself permission to no longer run on empty, however, when you attempt to give of yourself to your circle in your current environment. You do not have to live that way anymore. It is too tiresome, too stressful, and quite frankly, totally unfair to you.

One more thing, look at those in your environment. Do they all need you to continually give of yourself all of the time? Can anyone in the circle step up and do a little more so that you can step down and do a little less, or are you still controlling that? They take and not give because you make it that way. You have convinced everyone and yourself that it has to be you to take care of everything because they need and depend on you, yes? They do not know how to do it like you, right? They can not function without you, true? You have to explore why you sabotage yourself to be depended upon by your circle. What is the precipitating factor that is driving you to self-sabotage? Explore this and write it down in your journal. When you pinpoint the culprit that is driving you to do and to be all to everyone, then please give yourself permission to stop. Awareness is always the key to empowering one's self. Yes, this is easier said than done. But it is worth it. *You* are worth it.

**Self-Sabotaging**

Would you like a basis as to know where self-sabotaging originates? There are times we wear *masks* in public to cover up what we determined as unacceptable and dreadful about ourselves. We need to be bold and acknowledge the different masks that we wear, and explore how these masks benefit and take away from being our true selves. Understandably, the mask is all you know. But do you realize that there comes a point in which you no longer need to wear it? You never really needed to. Toward the end of this book I will help you take off the mask for good to begin getting accustomed to life without it. Take note at how relieved, happy, and successful you will be in making this conscious and wise decision to take off your mask!

**The 3 Masks**

First and foremost, we need to identify the masks we wear. Let's begin with an overview of the masks we put on. They are called, *The Pretty Mask, The Performer Mask, and the Dark Mask.* My prototypes in relation to the 3 totalities of the Self were extracted from teachings by my former professors, Dr.

Sheldon Nix and his colleagues, when I was in my Master's Degree Program at Eastern University in Pennsylvania.

**Pretty Mask.** *The Pretty Mask* is the external mask. It is the mask that everyone sees with the naked eye. This is the mask which we display to the world. For instance, you may want people to know you as a hard worker who is motivated, ambitious, and hard driven. You are praised and recognized for your achievements, and acknowledged as a go-getter in your field.

**Performer Mask.** *The Performer Mask* is the mask that performs and protects. Let's say that you are secretly a slacker, and out of the millions of people who love and adore you for your ambition and drive, there is that one person who contests that you are not as ambitious or as hard driven as you portray. It is always that one person for whom we will desperately up our game and double our efforts in order to shut up the naysayer. In order to prevent being exposed as a fraud, your *Desperate Mask* attempts to divert and distract people from discovering your slacker side by showing how much more ambitious and driven you are. You will offer and over-extend yourself to your job, business, friends, and family just to prove that you are truly what people say and know you to be, based on what you present to them as a *Pretty Mask.* You do this all to avoid your *Dark Mask.*

**Dark Mask.** It is your *Dark Mask* that is the core issue, yet, it is a place to which no one ventures. Your *Pretty* and *Performer Masks* tirelessly work together to cover up the *Dark* persona, which can be a number of things. In this example, the *Dark Mask* would be a self-perception of *Insignificance, Worthlessness, and Being Nothing.* You subconsciously believe that this is your true self, being insignificant, worthless, and nothing. You seemingly pretend at the *Pretty Mask* level to be opposite of the *Dark Mask Level.* You attempt to do things at the *Dark Mask* level to keep people from discovering the *Dark Mask* when others are not convinced or impressed at the *Pretty Mask* level.

Overall, this is such a tiresome, depleting, and draining cycle in which to live. This illustration demonstrates low and unhealthy self-esteem. This way of life is quite empty and unfulfilling. But it is a matter of reframing it all and seeing your true worth. Here's how.

## The Truth about the Masks

Truthfully, your *Pretty Mask is* your true self. You are not pretending and you are not faking it. The problem is that you are *acting* instead of *being.* You thought to put on a mask because you believed that no one would accept you or your hang-ups. You pretty yourself up to the point of acceptance and approval. But are you fully accepted and approved? You may find yourself upset with loved ones who love the image you portray instead of the real person behind the portrayal. You may be upset with yourself because this is all you know, and you desire love and acceptance at the cost of being true and real. It is a never-ending and vicious cycle to continue living like that. Please give yourself permission to love yourself first. Accept *you,* first. Build up your self-esteem and worth. You have to love *you* before anyone else follows suit. Give yourself permission to just *Be.* Period. You will be so that happy you did. It will be like a weight lifted off your shoulders, and you will find it more effortless to live life with this new found freedom rather than to struggle living up to any and all expectations. Life is already hard in and of itself, please don't continue to add to life's hard knocks. Once you realize that the *Dark Mask* is *FEAR*, or **F**alse **E**vidence **A**ppearing **R**eal, then you will let go of this *Dark Mask* and live out as a *Real Self.* You will have the opportunity to live life to the fullest as it was designed to be lived. You will be more energized, more empowered, more confident, more centered, more grounded, and in more order! You will be much more respectful of your boundaries and hold others accountable and responsible to respect them, too. You will finally be ok with putting the oxygen mask on first, and then others' next. You will be ok to leave your corporate job to start your own catering business. You will be ok to leave your verbally abusive husband to live your life free from verbal abuse. You will be ok kicking your 30-year-old son, daughter-in-law, grandkids, and his mother-in-law out of your home so that you can be free to live your life without guilt or worry. You will be that much happier and successful, and will definitely be a force to be reckoned with. All of this and more can be yours if you first start giving yourself permission to dream it, taste it, smell it, feel it, breathe it, see it, and then to ultimately live it. *It's your turn to live life on your own terms.*

Now that you realized the masks that you wore and how you self-sabotaged, you now need to know how to address your mindset to stop wearing the masks and stop the self-sabotaging.

### Steps for Addressing Self-Talk

First, explore and then challenge your thinking. Your brain will attempt to protect you from making any changes in your life or pursuing your happiness and success with thoughts of: *"They need me!" "I'm ok, I can handle my responsibilities and still care for them." "If I don't do for them then something will happen and it will be all my fault!" "They cannot do it like me anyway." "They cannot function or live without me."*

Next, write down all the self-talk that you do in your head so that you can see them all. Then, question all of your self-talk: *"Do they really need me, because Junior is 30 and making 6 figures and he, his wife and the twins really don't need to live with Tom and I anymore, or live off of our retirement money."*

*"Can I really handle my responsibilities without putting off my doctor's appointment again?" "Will something fall on my watch and it really be my fault?" "Why? That is what Tom is for! To help me with our kids!" "Can they not really function without me? They seem to function when I am called away for business once a quarter! My house is still intact, nothing turned off, and they were able to make dinner for themselves..... hmmmmm."*

Yes! I want you to really think about this. Write down the self-talk, explore where it comes from, and then challenge those statements. You will be happy that you did.

### Case Study: Me

Give yourself permission to be happy and successful. There are no limits except the ones you set for yourself. This is a lesson that I learned early on. I justified not starting my own businesses because I was young, a woman, poor, had an ailing parent, etc. etc. etc. That's life for you! Life is going to do its part. We have to do ours. I continued to create my businesses despite these issues. Lessons were learned, and so I do what the late great author, Maya Angelou, said to do, "...*When you learn, teach.*" With each step that I made, I had to give myself permission to change my attitude and actions. I did not grow up in a home of business owners, and was not around business owners at all. I had to learn all of this on my own, and so I did. During my Master's Degree journey, I claimed one of my clinical supervisor's as my favorite supervisor because she decided to stop working for the company that I interned (which I was inevitably fired from later on.... yes, I know) to start her own private practice. In my own clinical private practice, I normally shared with my internship mentees that it is better to sit under a mentor who is doing what you aspire to do. Looking back, when I was a student, I realized that I could not necessarily learn from a supervisor who is not self-employed if being self-employed is what I aspired to be someday. So I followed my clinical supervisor, Linda, to her private practice and the game changed for me. I had to pay her more for clinical supervision, and be on time for the sessions or forfeit them. I appreciated Linda greatly because her teaching and mentorship helped me to create my future clinical private practice, RESET, LLC. I was licensed in multiple states and established clinical practices on the East Coast. I had directly and indirectly impacted thousands of lives over the years through my very own company! I had to first give myself permission and the green light to make this totally unfamiliar and uncomfortable move. I had plenty of opposition and plenty of reasons not to start my own business, but I placed more weight on the fear of not having any income to pay the bills, not to mention moving back home and dealing with my dad and brothers, than I did in dealing with the opposition and naysayers. As I mentioned, it was a lesson learned. I would not encourage anyone to be motivated by fear in doing anything. It can be a physical, mental, and emotional wear and tear to which you may not recover from, and could result in an inability to enjoy the benefits earned from accomplishing your goals. While in a state of fear and worry, do it anyway. In other words, take action through the process of SMART and SIMPLE goals, which as a bonus chapter, I will teach you how to set goals to obtain your happiness and success!

In the meantime, pursue your goals by the benefits that you will reap and let the results be your motivating factors. It is a matter of being laser focused on the goal, and to have a '*No Matter What Attitude*' like Motivational Speaker and best-selling author, Lisa Nichols has said. Be clear on your pursuit to happiness and success. Know what you are working towards so that you can stay on track; otherwise, you will be spinning your wheels by not knowing if you have even accomplished the goal! Move your daydream of turning left at the fork in the road from being just a dream to becoming actual and real for you. Take action to make it happen. You can do this!

**Give yourself permission to do so.**

# Exercise Activity: An Affirmation for the Spirit

*Remember to Acknowledge, Embrace, and Accept You! Declare an affirmation and declaration over your spirit and soul. After reading this affirmation aloud, think of what other affirmations you want to declare. Pay attention to any feelings that rise up within you. You may write these down below.*

*Examples: I declare peace in my spirit today. I declare my emotions are healed and whole today. I declare I am no longer suffering from hurt in my spirit/soul today. I declare I am not overwhelmed today! I declare I am not broken to pieces, but totally at peace today! I declare it is well in my soul today! I declare I will start listening to my inner self and obey it today!*

_____

_____

_____

_____

_____

_____

# **Reflection Activity**: *Self- Esteem*

*Find a quiet space to reflect on these questions before moving to the next chapter. Write your answers here.* Reflect on these questions, and answer with an honest heart. Your responses will help you along your journey.

How is your self-esteem?

_____
_____
_____
_____
_____

How much do you really value yourself?

_____
_____
_____
_____
_____

Do you place your value and worth on approval, acceptance, and love by others? In what way?

_____
_____
_____
_____
_____

Do you love yourself? Is so, how do you show it? If not, how come?

_____

_____

_____

_____

_____

# Chapter 6: YOU ARE THE MISSING LINK

*"Be patient. Just like a puzzle, it takes time for all the pieces of your life to come together."*
**Anonymous-Taken from Pintrest.com**

What is missing in your equation? All the players that perhaps should *no longer* be players on your field of life are all present and accounted for. Yet, the Most Valuable Player is missing. The star quarterback is not here! Where is she? Who is she? That MVP I am talking about is of course, *You!* I believe that we are often the missing link in our own equation. You are the missing link to fulfilling your goal of ultimate happiness and success. All that you need is within you, just as was discussed in Chapter Four.

### Case Study: Me

I listened to my parents' wishes for me, and I lived out dreams that they likely wanted for themselves. I went to school, had my own house, car, business, and without having children out of wedlock, without going to jail, and without having any extra baggage in my life. Yet, I was not entirely happy. I felt

91

something was horribly missing. I did not pursue the artsy side of me. I did not go into singing or fashion design. I felt that a part of me had either died or did not have a chance to fully live. I was living out my parents' dreams and not my dreams. It was my choice, however, although I initially blamed my parents for my unhappiness. I had to mature and take ownership for my decisions because I realized blaming others did not rectify or resolve anything. Blaming others and not taking ownership for my decisions actually kept the cycle going. I chose to complete my PhD program with the intention of closing out my debts to my parents in upholding the family name. Once I finished my degree, I jokingly told everyone, "That's it! Here are my Emancipation papers, I am no longer a slave to the Langley family. It's now time to get knocked up, barefoot and pregnant! I am open for business!" I had the nerve to post that on Facebook! You should have seen the inbox message inquiries! Seriously, I was so happy to complete my program so that I could finally live my life on my own terms! And guess what? On the day that I returned from commencement, I had to not only continue to care for my mother who has late stage Alzheimer's Disease, but I had now inherited my dad to live with me and care for him, too! Talk about Karma! I thought I was done living for others and that it was *My Turn Now*! Interestingly, it was *My Turn Now*. My point here is that we cannot predict what life brings. It is not a matter of going after your happiness when your last child leaves home for college, because your child can always come back home. It is not a matter of going after your success once you retire from your job of 30 years, because you may have to go back to work a month later after you have retired. Regardless of what life brings, *Your Turn Starts Now!*

I have accepted what life presented to me, and while what's been presented to me has been painful to say the least, I am still pursuing my happiness and my success. While caring for my parents, I wrote this book. I closed out RESET, LLC to rebrand myself and start over in my new business venture. I travel more than I've ever had. Regardless of what life threw at me, I was determined to have *My Turn Now, Darnit!* I implore you to do the same, regardless of where you are in your life.

Who said that you can't have your turn now while attending to your obligations? You will come to realize that you do not need to manage all of the responsibilities you have on your plate. You can let go of some or most of them to make room, energy, and time for you. I am not saying that you should be neglectful toward your responsibilities. But you need to analyze and assess which ones no longer belong on your plate. Analyze and assess the reasons why you still carry them. If it is to feel better about yourself, your self-worth, and your self-esteem, then it is time for you to build your self-worth and self-esteem by accepting and loving yourself to the fullest! It is time for you to embrace that other part of you that you had buried and kept hidden because that part of you can no longer be contained. You can no longer be the missing link to your equation. It is time to be whole, full, and complete. *It is Your Turn Now to Live Life* to the fullest extent imaginable*!* Get rid of any old, dead and excess weight in your life *Now*! Give yourself permission to do so.

It's Your Turn NOW!

**Happiness and Success Story: Halle Berry**

I love reading about the Oscar Winning Actress Halle Berry. Halle Berry has often shared her humble beginnings before stardom, which included being homeless at one point. In her early 20s, Halle Berry was on her way to Chicago, and with little to no money, she reached out to her mother for more. Her mother made the decision that it would be best not to send her any money. During these tough times, Halle has said that she lived in a homeless shelter. In an interview, Berry shared:

*"It taught me how to take care of myself and that I could live through any situation, even if it meant going to a shelter for a small stint, or living within my means, which were meagre. I became a person who knows that I will always make it my own way."*

This is the type of mindset you must have in order to press forward in your pursuit of happiness and success. Ms. Berry didn't recognize her strength and resilience until she was in a situation to recognize these great attributes. She was able to discover herself and no longer remain missing, which became evident in her acting career and ultimate success as an Oscar Winner.

Likewise, know that the light at the end of the tunnel is great, it is bright, and it is waiting for you. There may have been people that you were perfectly designed to help and assist, but there are also people perfectly designed to help and assist you. They are along the path of your happiness and success journey. Please make room for them, and discard the people, places, and things you no longer need to have or carry along your individual path. You are at a unique place and time in your life to be strong and steadfast, focused and determined, unwavering and courageous. Yes, courageous. It takes absolute courage to truly be yourself in this world. And you are courageous! I am proud of you for taking the first action step in recognizing that you are the missing link in your equation. And I am certainly proud of you for taking the next action steps, which were getting this book and actually reading this book! Thanks for not having this book as a Shelf-Help Book!

It's Your Turn NOW!

## Happiness and Success Story: Tory Burch

Tory Burch, CEO and Designer of Tory Burch LLC, began her career in the late 1980's in the fashion industry, often working as a writer or in the area of public relations and advertising. She had opportunities to work with well-known fashion names, such as Vera Wang and Ralph Lauren. Then in 2004 she began her own fashion label, and has quickly become a success. Burch usually proclaimed that success never happens overnight, and that success instead is a grueling cycle of successes and failures which then lead to bigger successes. Her motto was success happens one step at a time.

In Burch's 2014 commencement speech at Babson College, she told graduates, *"By following your passion, the path you've embarked on is truly exciting, but it can also be challenging. Here's what life has taught me, being an entrepreneur isn't just a job title, and it isn't just about starting a company. It's a state of mind. It's about seeing connections others can't, seizing opportunities others won't, and forging new directions that others haven't. It's about being entrepreneurial wherever you are and in whatever you do. It's about having the courage to follow your passion about an idea that makes your heart race. If it doesn't scare you, you're probably not dreaming big enough...."*

Ms. Burch is right. Have the courage to follow your passion and purpose even if it makes you fearful, uncomfortable, and scared. It's time to be daring, tenacious, and even down right ruthless about your happiness and success! Your efforts toward your happiness and success will not be in vain. Plow through all of the obstacles, situations, and circumstances just like you have for the sake of everyone else. I would love for you to show yourself that same courtesy in order to accomplish your goals of being happy and being successful.

**Happiness and Success Story: Anita Roddick**

Anita Roddick is the founding director and CEO of a popular British cosmetics company, The Body Shop. Roddick, who died in 2007, was an activist and champion for social causes and environmental issues. She was quite resourceful and was savvy with the way she met the needs of the community.

Roddick was definitely a risk taker and a positive thinker with a deep desire to achieve the impossible while defying all odds. She is known for her creativity and innovation in the beauty world.

Anita was in touch with her passions in life, particularly after some time working with the United Nations and travels throughout the world. She decided to blend together her passions with business, and founded The Body Shop, which was a small shop in its infancy. In the beginning, she had difficulty getting a bank loan in order to open the shop. But Anita never gave up. Her husband believed in her dream, and together they began forming their shop. There were mistakes along the way, but Anita held tight to her goals and before long she found her way. The Body Shop was the first cosmetic company to market products not tested on animals, and Anita helped pave the way for organic, green-living products, which have become quite popular now. The Body Shop soon became a franchise business, and employs more than 22,000 people in 60 countries around the world.

Roddick actualized her dream. She had a vision and she recognized that the only way to actualize her vision into reality was to no longer be a missing link to the equation. She had passion, purpose, and desire that went beyond making money. She saw the bigger picture. Likewise, in your own life, try to see the bigger picture. It is not merely about being happy and successful. But it is about being totally whole, complete, and fulfilled. It is about finally living life to the fullest and finding out in the process that it is very possible to live as such. It is about *being*, and not just existing. It is about appreciating the process throughout the journey, and finally finding yourself. It is about learning and sharing, and teaching afterwards. It is all about *You*. Fill your own void, do not seek others to fill it. Continually move forward and breathe, sleep, and eat your goals of happiness and success. You will indirectly motivate others to discover their missing links, too.

### Final Thoughts: I was the Missing Link

I had realized that while I was the missing link to my equation, whatever was to happen in my life was scheduled to happen, with or without my consent. I played small for too long during my time as a Licensed Professional Counselor. I was too afraid to step out and become a self-pay counseling practice because I didn't know how to market, sell, or promote my services. In my opinion, I was a slave to managed care organizations. I allowed managed care to dictate my prices, my clients, and ultimately, my financial worth. It was tiresome. I was worried about paying my bills and living expenses when the insurance companies delayed or denied my psychotherapy claims for the services rendered to my clients. But I had noticed that I never had an eviction notice, foreclosure, car repossession, or went without food. In caring for my parents, they never went without anything they needed, and I was still on my meagre counseling salary. I had very little money, yet it worked out for me to travel, build my new business, and take care of all of my financial and personal obligations. How? My calling, purpose, and destiny were not predicated by my checkbook whatsoever. It was predicated by my faith to believe in God, and to believe in myself.

There's a saying, whatever will be, will be. If it is meant for you to be happy, to live life to the fullest, to live a purpose-filled life beyond the roles and titles you have, then it will all come to pass. And I will dare say regardless of you making it happen or not, it will come to pass! You can't even stop the purpose and calling on your life! I have attempted to avoid many things in my life. Yet it was inevitable for it to all happen. Why? That's how God made it to be for my life. I will get personal here, as I am a total open book. Do you recall me saying earlier that we do not have weaknesses, just uncultivated strengths? Well, we are born with gifts and talents. These gifts and talents have to go through life's challenges in order to grow, mature, and activate. These gifts are not solely for us; they are to help and to be a blessing to others. I believe that we have these gifts and talents but we were once clueless on how to use them correctly. These gifts must be fostered and cultivated, just like flower seeds. Unfortunately, a lack of understanding and knowledge of our gifts and talents can result in abuse, misuse, and inactivation of our unique abilities. I have had unspeakable things happen to me in my life, and I have done unspeakable things in my life. The things that have happened in my life seemed inevitable in my mind, regardless of how hard I've tried to prevent those things from happening. I thought I avoided the inevitable, but I lied to myself, pretending that I wasn't doing things that, in essence, resulted in those unspeakable things happening. I do not blame myself for all of the things that have happened to me. However, it is no longer about blame or criticism. It is about maturity, humility, growth, and gratitude. I can beat myself up for entering into an abusive relationship when I was a teenager. I can blame the perpetrator who raped me just before I got into the car with my parents, who were taking me to my first day of college. I can blame my Daddy for not regarding or protecting me. I can go on, and on, and on! But blaming does not change what happened. I have learned to stop pretending that I wasn't doing the things that got me into trouble, and started taking ownership for my reactions and behaviors. I gave up being the victim and claimed the parts I played in the unfavorable situations so that I could learn, grow, and move on to now teach others what to look out for and what not to do. I had repented to God and asked Him for another chance to get it right, and to live my life the way He planned and created it. I am eternally grateful to live life and to embrace all that it brings, the good and the bad, whatever is classified as good and as bad. I am in a unique position to care for both parents, and to be a blessing to both of them as they both have been a blessing to me. My mother, in particular, despite this stupid disease robbing her mind, has not robbed her spirit nor her essence. I continually receive my strength and endurance by watching her endure and choose to live every single day. She could choose to die and no longer deal with Alzheimer's Disease. Yet, as I looked at these things as a negative, perhaps she is most appreciative of living life up to the minute. She is still here at the time of writing this book, whereas many of her loved ones have already passed on. I am grateful for life, and to live life. It is wrong not to live life as intended and designed.

When I realized I was the missing link to my own equation, suddenly, I recognized the open doors and opportunities for my happiness and my success. The unspeakable things I have done in my life were no longer issues, because I occupied my time doing things I loved to do and enjoy. I didn't have to fill anymore voids, as I started discovering who I really was. And it was an amazing discovery.

Now that I have found my missing link, I knew I had to help others find their missing links. Therefore, I started writing this book as a newly PhD graduate with the hopes to inspire and uplift successful women who may have felt overlooked, disregarded, or unappreciated, and who may have felt rather unsuccessful or unhappy with their lives. I share my story of hope and persistence to demonstrate all things can truly be possible as long as you believe. I have helped thousands of women over the course of my Clinical Psychotherapy career to deal with abuse, rape, injustice, and mistreatment. I have also helped thousands of women boost their esteem, love themselves first, regard themselves as the missing and important link to their equation, and to establish courtesy, self-respect, order, and boundaries for their lives. On top of all of this, I have the unique pleasure to inform women all over the world *that It Is Their Turn Now,* and the duty to empower them *to Live Life on Their Own Terms!*

## Steps To No Longer Be The Missing Link

I implore you to no longer be the missing link in your equation. Include yourself. Live your life while managing your roles and obligations. You can do this. Regardless of what you have or do not have, living your life happy and successful is not predicated by your possessions. You were already wonderfully made with the gifts and talents bestowed to you. But you need to truly find out who you really are. Instead of allowing your brain to protect you, and you going through the motions based on the negative things your parents, kids, spouse, friends, boss or employees have said about you, go by what you say about yourself. What do you really say about you beyond the masks, the *Pretty Mask,* the *Performer Mask,* the *Dark Mask*? What do you really say about *you*? *Who are You?* In order to really take the time to learn all there is to know about you, please *reorder* yourself. As mentioned before, give yourself permission to no longer be the missing link. Your time is *Now*. Your time is Here.

It is *Your Turn Now* to Live Life On Your Own Terms! Don't worry about past attempts that you deemed as failures. Say, "*It's ok. That was then and this is Now.*" Pick yourself up and try again. No longer allow yourself to feel or be empty and unfulfilled. Your previous plans may not have materialized, but re-strategize, that's all! Fill your voids with purpose, filled with happiness and success. If that means your happiness lies in being a seamstress, a photographer, a Fashion Designer (ahem), or whatever your heart's desire, listen to your inner voice! That part of you that was missing or hidden, let that part of you shine, even if it totally contradicts your current role or lifestyle. Instead of looking at it negatively, look at it positively. Who said you can't do what is in your heart while maintaining your current lifestyle? Just start! You may be surprised that your heart's desire inevitably overshadows your current lifestyle. In fact, your heart's desire may actually afford you an even better lifestyle, greater success, and happiness overall, because all of you is in it now. You are great at what you do even at only 60%!

How much greater and successful could you be if you were at 100%? By percentage, I mean being fully and wholly present. Challenge yourself! Look for mentors or read autobiographies about your favorite people. If you have a favorite celebrity, thought leader, mentor, or person whom you admire, follow their humble beginnings. Notice that many of our Sheroes had tragedies and disadvantages. Yet they, by no means, allowed tragedies or disadvantages to stop them. They used them to their advantage, and these challenges only fueled their successes. Raise the bar for yourself. Set your goals for what will make you happy and successful. Know what happiness looks like for you. In fact, create a vision board! A vision board is a visual board that you create based on what you want to accomplish. Some people cut out pictures of those desired goals and paste them onto a board as a visual reminder. You can create a digital one with audio. You may not be a visual and kinaesthetic learner like me, so whatever works to help you learn, please make it fun and fascinating! Additionally, start listening to self-help audios and attend motivational conferences to help connect with other likeminded people. Remember to create a new environment that serves as a safe space for you, and surround yourself with an amazing circle of people who can help you grow and attain your goals toward happiness and success.

For the sake of being realistic, however, please know and accept that as your success did not come overnight, your happiness will also not come overnight. Please do not have unrealistic expectations about your happiness and success to the point that you self-sabotage and justify not pursuing it simply because your success and happiness aren't happening as expected or as planned. Again, you have to be real and truthful with yourself. Remember what I said about searching your feelings, thoughts, and actions, and reviewing how you plan to achieve your happiness and success. All of the right elements need to be in place for you to successfully achieve your goals. There will be lessons learned in the journey that are worth notating. You know it will take continuous effort on your part, and that life will happen along the way. But let life happen, that's its job. Your job is to continue onward, and all the while you will grow, enhance, and further improve along the journey. Remember, this is *your* journey, *your* passion, and *your* desire. Everyone may not celebrate your decision in your journey of being happy and successful. And it is perfectly *OK.* You are not doing it for them. You are doing it for yourself.

You are the missing link, that bright star in the darkness. I heard once that instead of cursing the darkness, simply light a candle to it. Lighting your candle by way of pursuing your own happiness and success will make a tremendous difference and an indelible mark in this world. We need you. Add yourself to the equation so that the equation is finally complete. You have figured your way out of so many things for the sake of others, now do the same for yourself. Just as the Bible says, do not despise small beginnings, and be not weary in doing well. You are one of excellence, and are very relevant for today. You are independent, driven, passionate, and possess the capacity to be happy and successful.

***No longer be the missing link to your equation.***

# Exercise Activity: An Affirmation "Release & Let Go"

*Form five affirmations, and then write these down here.*

*I AM*……….. (the one thing you discovered that you are talented, creative, and innovative)

_____
_____
_____
_____
_____
_____
_____

*I CHOOSE*……(the one thing you commit to do going forward)

_____
_____
_____
_____
_____
_____
_____

*I BELIEVE*…..(your new and changed view of yourself)

_____
_____
_____
_____
_____
_____
_____

*I FORGIVE*…..(Repeat this as necessary, & You may also say, I CHOOSE TO HAVE COMPASSION FOR ……)

_____
_____
_____
_____
_____
_____
_____

*I DECLARE*….. (one thing you want to see happen and change….shape your mindset to prepare and gravitate to what you want to see)

_____
_____
_____
_____
_____
_____
_____

***And then declare, I release and let it all go! I am now healed, free, released, forgiven, at peace, and am whole!***

# Reflection Activity: *I Declare*

In your journal write this phrase at the top of the page, "*MY DECLARATIONS.*" Date it for today. Log a daily entry of an aspiration which you declare to accomplish as it pertains to your goals of happiness and success. Make it personal, and be bold, courageous, and confident as you list your *Declarations* for the next 30 days. At the end of 30 days, you have just created your first book of *Declarations*! You can share it with others, keep it to yourself, create a blog page surrounding it, create audio to go along with it, or whatever you want to do with it. It is yours to use and repurpose for the rest of your life and beyond! You will immediately shift to the top percentage of elite women who creates declarations for themselves.

If you want to take it a step further, journal your thoughts, feelings and reactions surrounding the creation of your daily declarations. Categorize the *Top 5 Declarations*, from greatest to least, to determine which declarations have the most significant impact in attaining your goals of happiness and success. After 30 days, make it a point to start your declarations with the Top 5 read first, and then the remaining ones all on the same day. Carve out 10 minutes to read all of your declarations each and every morning before doing anything else. You will be empowering yourself to stay focused and to finish strong. We have learned to get to the finish line, but it is a matter of crossing the finish line for your happiness and your success

# Chapter 7: LET IT ALL FALL

*"Never be afraid to fall apart because it is an opportunity to rebuild yourself the way you wish you had been all along."*
**Rae Smith**

This is my favorite chapter. Numerically, seven means completion. I originally had eight secrets, for which the number eight signifies new beginnings. I wanted to help bring you to completion before helping you to start a new chapter in your life, so that you can do the most important parts when completing any goal or task; *celebrate, reflect, and rest!* Take a moment to celebrate that you made it through this book! Yay! Now reflect on what you have learned or received in reading this book. What resonated most with you? Why do you think that resonated most with you? What made you feel uncomfortable? Why you do think that it did? What challenged you and caused you more confusion? Why do you think that happened?

I have learned from Robert Riopel, one of my favorite trainers at New Peaks, that being in confusion, and I am paraphrasing, is the best place to be, because it evokes you to think, makes you become aware, and challenges you in your comfort zone. I hope I confused you! Additionally, I am about to challenge you and make you feel even more uncomfortable and confused. Ready? Ok.

Think about your current responsibilities and obligations. Why do they exist? Why are they on your plate? It is amazing how you wear multiple hats, whether the hats were passed down to you, or you decided to put the hats on, all at the same time might I add. You have plenty of accessories to choose from which to adorn and accentuate your features. Ask yourself if your accessories deflect or distract away from seeing any flaws that you think you may have? Do you wear makeup to enhance and show off your beauty, or do you use makeup to hide blemishes, dark spots and scars? It is said that the clothes make the person. But do you wear black clothes to give an appearance of a slimmer figure, and avoid anything form fitting because it will really show your real shape? We cannot forget the shoes. Whose shoes are you really wearing? This is an introduction to my next book, *Just Get Naked: Accept and Embrace The True*

*Skin You're In!* I identify the various ways which we attempt to deceive, distract, and deflect what we perceive as negative and unacceptable away from ourselves, while struggling with self-acceptance and overall self-significance. I discuss how to acknowledge, embrace, and accept the real you by using analogies to which we can relate. As a teaser, I will begin talking about the multiple hats that we wear from my next book, as it relates to this chapter.

## Multiple Hats from Just Get Naked Book

Do you like hats? I do. I love stylish hats. I love how adding a hat into my ensemble adds flavor, style, and pizzazz to my look. Hats are to cover your head, and serve to protect and provide comfort. However, hats, as discussed here, represent the roles and responsibilities that we have. Many, if not all of us, wear a hats simultaneously based on multiple factors. We wear multiple hats because the hats were inherited, passed down, or even forced on us to wear. At times, we wear hats that do not fit us, that are too big and too heavy to balance on our heads. Also, some hats that we wear are like having a life sentence; the punishment is that these hats swallow us up, smother, or suffocate us. Sadly, we regret the multiple hats we have because the hats do not add flavor, style, or pizzazz to our lives. The hats do not protect or cover. These hats add wear and tear to our lives, and they emotionally, mentally, and physically drain us from time to time. Overall, wearing these hats is a total detriment to us. We have convinced ourselves that the multiple hats we were is at the benefit of those for whom we wear them, such as for our family, our job, and our community, and it is unfortunately at our expense. We often reframe our perspective about wearing the multiple hats and conclude that wearing these hats make us stronger and wiser. We also believe it is in the cards for us; it is an inevitable part of our existence. You probably wish you could lose the hat somewhere, that someone would even steal your hats, or that you could give them back to the original owner! But you then acquiesce, and think that maybe it's you, or that you aren't wearing these hats correctly. You attempt to readjust the hats because you have convinced yourself that you are not seeing the bigger picture, and that you should be grateful that you have these hats and that you can juggle so many at the same time. You think that those in your life could not wear or juggle multiple hats like you do, and so you resume wearing all of the hats that you own for the betterment of those to whom you are responsible. Here's the biggest issue, juggling multiple hats on your head looks silly, even though many praise you and are amazed at how you can juggle them all. It goes beyond the praise and admiration. You have to look at how it is impacting your life. You are worth more than mere praise and admiration. Why isn't anyone else juggling all those hats on their heads? It is not because they cannot, they are just smart enough not to! In other words, you are taking on more responsibilities than what you were supposed to, and more than you were built for! You may think that no one can juggle the roles and responsibilities like you, or that others would mess up in taking such huge responsibilities, or that those roles and responsibilities were designed for you to carry and juggle. Consequently, it is about balance. Not a balancing act. It is about balance in terms of everyone holding their own weight.

Being praised and adored are a thing of the past. You are overwhelmed, stressed out, maxed out, and burnt out from juggling these hats without help. Juggling these hats are a determinant to your health, admit it! In fact, let's be clear. You are not one person juggling multiple hats. You are a different person based on what each particular hat calls for you to be. You have a Business Hat, Significant Other Hat, Grown Up-Child Hat, and a Faux Hat!

**Business Hat.** You are given all the responsibilities at your job when you wear the Business Hat. You are reliable, dependable, hard-working, and no one can wear this hat like you. You find it hard to say no, and also find it difficult to delegate responsibilities and duties to your team. As a result, you suffer from the *Donna Do It All Syndrome*! If you wish to learn more about the signs, symptoms, and strategies to combat the *Donna Do It All Syndrome*, please take my Free Destress To Success Quiz at www.sarahreneelangley.com .

**Significant Other Hat.** Your Significant Other Hat gives you a sense of pride and accomplishment to manage your family duties, spousal duties, and even daughter duties to your retired, elderly parents. You have been able to juggle many responsibilities and multiple roles throughout the years despite the struggles, challenges, personal setbacks and sacrifices. You often wonder who else sacrificed. What do you have to show for your dedication, commitment, and sacrifice to your family? Why were you chosen to be the sacrifice? What do you get out of it? You feel guilty for having these thoughts, but nevertheless, you have them. You have convinced yourself that if you do not pull this hat off then it will be at the detriment of your family. You believe you cannot let that happen, *not on your watch.* Perhaps you wonder what life would have been like if you had made that left turn at the fork in the road of life instead of listening to everyone. You often feel lonely, isolated, and forgotten. You wonder if you are really regarded, respected, or appreciated for all that you do and have sacrificed. If any of this resonates with you, you suffer from the *Linda Lonely Syndrome*! If you wish to learn more about the signs, symptoms, and strategies to combat the *Linda Lonely Syndrome*, please take my Free DeStress to Success Quiz at www.sarahreneelangley.com .

**Grown Up-Child Hat.** Your Grown Up-Child Hat is an interesting hat. Have you ever heard of the expression, *'A child trapped in an adult's body?'* Well, you are an adult trapped in a child's body. Do you remember your very first physical hat when you were a child? How did you look? How did you feel? How old were you? How did it fit? What caused you to wear it? Was it for an event? Do you realize the very first hat you wore set the tone for wearing future hats and roles and obligations, and responsibilities? When I was a little girl, my very first hat was a bonnet to go with my Easter dress when I was about 5 or 6 years old. It was white, and I had lace gloves, lace socks, and black shoes with lace on them. My dress was white with some type of pretty embroidery and appliques, and my pocketbook had some type of lace on it, too. I had to speak at the Easter Sunday service where I was to read a passage from the Bible, and I decided to up the ante by memorizing it so as to stand out amongst the crowd. And I did stand out. The passage that I chose, which eerily enough has been my go-to passage for years to come—*"Now Faith is the substance of things hoped for, the evidence of things not seen. Hebrews 11:1."* Oh, the standing ovation! The applause! That was the beginning of always wearing the perfect, beautiful hat that makes me stand out and get praise and attention. Coincidentally, this also was the beginning of taking on more than I could chew because it was always expected of me to be more advanced than others my age. I will give you an example.

## Case Study: Me

When I was 19 years old, my dad was told that he possibly had intestinal cancer and was in the hospital for weeks. During this time, there wasn't any money coming in to pay for any bills. My mom and brothers made an unfortunate financial decision that resulted in losing our home, and we became homeless. My brothers moved to Virginia and stayed with relatives to work on projects in an attempt to purchase our home back, while my parents stayed in a motel and I stayed with my best friend and her son. I was the 'smart one' in the family. It was always expected for me to excel, to advance, and to do the family proud, just like I did at 5 years old. I was tasked with the responsibilities to go to college, ride 2-4 hours back and forth to work, send money to my brothers in Virginia, pay for my parents to stay in the motel weekly, and also to earn my keep while living with my girlfriend. I slept on trash bags full of clothes, so I was often achy and sore in the morning, and very tired as I left for work around 4 am and returned home around midnight sometimes pulling doubles for more money. I was only 19.

I have always had responsibilities that were beyond what I should have handled, yet I took on the responsibilities for the praise, the applause, and for the admiration. I would wear this special hat for almost 20 years because, to this day, I still pay for everyone's expenses. I am a caregiver for both parents, and it is still expected of me to give money to my brothers! I definitely suffered from the *Yolanda Yes Syndrome* (if you would like to take my free DeStress To Success Quiz to determine if you, too, suffer from the Yolanda Yes Syndrome and need to know about the signs, symptoms, and strategies to combat this, please go to my website at www.sarahreneelangley.com). I found myself saying 'yes' to everything and everyone! This is why. A trauma had occurred when we lost our home, not to mention the trauma of possibly losing my father. Trauma is representative of an end or even a death to something. It was as if life as we knew it had ceased. Chronologically, we are all the age we are today in our number of years, but we are still stuck in time, and in my case, I was stuck at 19. The homeless situation was never fully addressed. It remained unanswered and devastating, to say the least. As a family, we never fully transitioned. It was challenging to transition on any account, especially since at the age of 19 I was transitioning from a young lady into an adult. Psychologically, all of this was too much for me to take and so part of my psyche stopped existing. I made a subconscious decision to put my life on hold because I interpreted that my family needed me and could not survive without me. I never married, and I do not have any children. I put my life on pause, and sometimes wondered when I would press play again. Today,

I receive overwhelming praise, admiration, and respect for my tireless caretaking efforts concerning my mom and my dad. Yet, respectfully, none of that matters now. For the first time in my life, I would gladly bypass the praise, applause, and admiration for a chance to press the play button. I would choose to forgo the attention, acceptance, and approval for a chance to live my life with a sense of fullness and purpose. I know that there is more to life than caring for my parents. There is a whole world to impact and inspire. Hence, the writing of this book.

Truth be told, if my mom could verbally tell me now, she never would have allowed me to do half of the things that I have done for my parents over the years if caring for them kept me from living life the way I was born to live it. This was the game changer for me that I just discovered last year while attending a New Peaks event. I realized that I did not accept what my mom expressed to me years before Alzheimer's Disease took hold of her. She once told me to live my life no matter what. My life is not meant to please my parents or anyone. She said there is so much more to my life than pleasing others and that I need to live it, and to be ok with that. She said that she would never want to be a burden to me if it was to hold up my life. I love my mommy! I realized at the New Peaks event that I didn't heed her words because she and my family had been in such a vulnerable state all those years before, and it was engrained in me to take care of them at my expense. When I finally embraced her words, I pressed play again!

I am cured from all syndromes! I welcome support and services to assist in caring for my parents when I am on travels. I delegate responsibility where necessary and needed so that it frees up my time, energy, and money to do other things that are important to me. I have a wonderful team supporting me in my business ventures, and I have strategic partners that help me in generating multiple streams of income. In a nutshell, I get to live life! *I LOVE MY LIFE!* My amazing mentor, Adam Markel, CEO of New Peaks, always encourages me to say and live by this. *I do love my life. Now.*

It's Your Turn NOW!

## My Real Reason Why I Wrote This Book For You

What I am about to personally share is with the hopes to relate to anyone reading this book. I skipped over *how* the multiple hats impacted me over the years. Would you like to know what state of mind I was in prior to finally having my *Aha moment and breakthrough*? Thanks for allow me to share and be an open book.

Wearing the multiple hats that I have had over the years and having experienced the different syndromes I previously mentioned pushed me to the point of the unthinkable. On Thursday, September 25th, 2014, I, Sarah Renee Langley, future PHD graduate, Licensed Professional Counselor of RESET, LLC, owner of multiple businesses, licensed in different states, Clinical Supervisor and mentor to other students, *was suicidal.* I was suicidal, and couldn't tell a soul that I was suicidal.

I no longer wanted to live. I felt so alone, as if God had forsaken me and my Mom. Out of all people, I did not understand why my Mom had to have Alzheimer's Disease, and I was tired of juggling her, the feud between my family and me because I was appointed Guardian of her Estate initially, managing my counseling practice as it struggled to survive from heavily reduced medical insurance reimbursements, dealing with a threat to go to court due to back pay owed to one of my assistants, and a strained relationship. To add to all of that, I felt even more guilty and ashamed because I was a therapist and I was having such thoughts! I couldn't tell anyone about it. I was alone in my home far away from everyone, and not a soul to reach out to. I cried out to God and expected Him to verbally say STOP! Guess what, God didn't 'say' anything! I was devastated! He was going to allow me to take my own life! I cried for about 3 hours that day alone in my house. With butcher knives on hand, I played back my entire life in my mind from the beginning to present. I tried to make sense of all of this, trying to figure out what went wrong and how and why I was in such a state that I was in. Honestly, not even believing that I was going to hell if I killed myself was going to stop me from killing myself! Wow! I was in a pretty bad place.

It's Your Turn NOW!

Yet, I mustered up enough strength to assess the entire situation. My inner self, which I call the Holy Spirit, said, *"You must really have a calling on your life for the Devil to want you to take yourself out of here. That's why you cannot take yourself out of here! You have great things to do on this Earth. You have to Live."* Time stood still at that very moment. I took a deep breath, exhaled, and called two of my girlfriends who were both ministers in their own right and I confessed that I was ready to kill myself and they better pray for me *Right Now!* They prayed up a storm that day. I felt relieved. I repented to God for thinking that I had the right to take the life that He has given, and to almost succumb to the pressures of life that I honestly put on myself for praise, acceptance, approval, and admiration. These factors motivated me and made me feel significant because my *Dreaded Mask* told me I was totally Insignificant, Worthless, Defective and Nothing. I had felt that way for most of my life. *Until Now.*

**What Helped Me Live My Life Now**

I shared this to relate to those who may be feeling suicidal or having suicidal thoughts right now. I do not knock you at all for feeling suicidal. While society labels suicide as a copout and a selfish and cowardly act, sadly, it is seen as an escape and a sense of freedom from the excruciating pain. I know, and can relate to the feeling. Relationship Expert, Dr. Harville Hendrix, discusses the idea of perforated exits in one of his books, Getting the Love You Want. While Hendrix uses perforated exits to explain a totally different concept in relation to relationships, I use the term perforated exits as a concept to explain how we often have means of escape from situations, regardless if those means are inevitably unhealthy, detrimental, or fatal. Perforated Exits represent boundaries, but these boundaries have tiny slits in them, making the boundaries very easily to bypass or in essence, *'slip through the cracks.'* How perforated are your boundaries, hmm? It's time to assess your boundaries, honor them, and fix them to be strong, solid, and protective. That's what I had to do.

It's Your Turn NOW!

**Victim or Victor.** With regards to being suicidal, I do not condone it, even as I can relate to it. My reason is because it is a matter of coming to yourself and realizing that you have more life left to live, and to believe that it can get better. It is your choice, bottom line, to be the victim or the victor. Please see beyond all the negative stuff and find the positives out of your life. Choose to be the Victor *now*.

**Find Your Inspiration.** What helped me through my struggles was also thinking about my mom. Not in the sense of me needing to stick around to take care of her, but in the sense of her being my inspiration. I found my inspiration in my Mom, who has late-stage Alzheimer's and is totally incapacitated and needs full-time care. Yet, she makes it a point to open her eyes every day and smile. I believe she appreciates living despite her condition. If *she* can appreciate her life, then me, who is able-bodied, can do the same, and do something with my life. And I did.

## Let It All Fall Now

Here's my answer for all of this nonsense. *Let It All Fall Now, Darnit!* Let all the hats fall off! Let all your responsibilities fall to the ground, and all your obligations fall off your plate! Let it all fall! *What? Did Dr. Sarah say that?! Oh, I am sorry, did I just give you a heart attack?* Yes, I said It! Here's why.

There is no reason for anyone else to jump in and save the day if you are always the one jumping in and saving the day every single day. Actually, doing this doesn't even speak to your character, your abilities, nor to your *Pretty Mask.* So why are you doing it all? You are hurting and sacrificing yourself unnecessarily, and not getting the appreciation, regard, or the thank yous that you may be secretly expecting and waiting on! It's too much, so stop it! Right Now! Why am I telling you to stop the madness? Here's why: You are human! I said, you are human! Say it with me and accept this fact: *"I Am Human."* It is Ok! Let it all fall!

It's Your Turn NOW!

Letting it all fall may be a silent way of rebellion, but can also be a silent cry for help, and quite honestly, a way of escape! Maybe you no longer want to be on the pedestal. Being on a pedestal is not all what it's cracked up to be! It is always expected for you to have the answers, to save the day, to lead the people, to cook, clean, wash dishes, help with homework, co-sign on the car, iron the socks, take the car to the shop, feed the babies, volunteer at the church, be the department head for the PTA, etc. etc. etc. You want a break. As a client of mine once said, it's like being on empty with 1,000 miles more to go. *To go on what?* If you let it all fall, oh, my word! Your family will suffer, you would let your team down, your job and the company will lose money, people will lose their jobs, the company will go bankrupt, your family will be homeless because it was your responsibility to bring in the money and take care of the bills, etc., etc., etc. What huge amounts of pressure to have on your shoulders! Is this all really true, that it will be all your fault? I think you are long overdue for a mind, body, and soul makeover! It is high time to finally do different and get different! It is time for you to let it all fall right now, so that you can take your turn now and live life on your own terms.

*Easier said than done, right?  I have the answer for you on how to turn this all around in order to be ultimately happy, healthy, and whole.  Let's do it!*

# **Reframe To Reflection Exercise**

First, I want to thank you for allowing me to be transparent, open, raw, real, and vulnerable with you. I am happy to share my experiences in hopes that by my self-disclosure, it motivates and inspires change, gives comfort and hope, and more importantly, empowers and propels you to seek a happy and successful life by recognizing your significance in this world. Thank you. Let's begin.

Get into a comfortable position wherever you are and sit upright. Close your eyes, take 3 deep breaths…a nice deep breath in, hold, and then exhale. Again, nice deep breath in, hold, then exhale. One more time, nice deep breath in, hold, then finally exhale. With your eyes closed, picture your life right now as it is.

Then, take a glimpse right now of what life would have been like if you had given yourself the chance to do what really makes you happy, to do what you really wanted. Let tears flow if they come, but do not stop this process. You need this for you *right now*.

Take deep breaths in, hold, then exhale. Take another deep breath in, hold, then exhale, and another breath in, hold, and finally exhale.

Notice how you are feeling. What are you seeing? What do you smell? What are you tasting? What do you hear right now? I want you to make practice of knowing yourself through all of your senses.

What would life have been like if you hadn't listened to Mom and had taken that job far away from home anyway? What would life have been like if you hadn't followed and supported your then-boyfriend now ex-husband to another continent because of what looked like a great job opportunity at the time, was a total bust and cost of your life savings? What would life have looked like if you hadn't married him or had the kids when you wanted to be a budding actress before saying, "I do"? What would life have been like if you had listened to him in the first place when he said he didn't want to have children, yet you are still married and childless?

# It's Your Turn NOW!

Take deep breaths in, hold, and then exhale out. Take another deep breath in, hold, and exhale out. One more time, take a deep breath in, hold, and exhale out.

How much happier would you be right now if you had listened to your inner self and not made that right turn at the fork in the road of your life? What did you gain by listening to everyone else and disrespecting your purpose and calling? By disrespecting your happiness and success?

Sacrifices do not always lead to huge gains. They leave great deficits. How much happier, satisfied, and fulfilled would you be if you had just trusted yourself, went against what everyone said, and be *you*?

Breathe in, hold, and breathe out. Breathe in, hold, and breathe out. Breathe in. Hold. And Breathe Out.

Now, I want you to quickly change the scene. With your eyes still closed, picture yourself today in real time. But you are smiling, you are happier, you are successful in the craft, skill, or role that you have chosen to do for your sake and not for others. You feel fulfilled, purposeful, whole, and at peace.

Take note of what you are wearing, the location, your thoughts at the moment, what you smell, hear, taste, see, and feel. This is free association time. Whatever comes to mind I want you to take mental notes.

I am helping you tap into the subconscious, as that is where our true answers lie. This is where the true direction for our lives resides. The subconscious mind is really what operates everything.

Whatever comes up for you, do not analyze, judge, disregard, or dismiss. Everything means something. Enjoy and appreciate yourself in your happy place. What do you see, think, or feel that plays a part in your happiness in that moment? Enjoy and relish this moment. You absolutely deserve it!

Take deep breaths in, hold, then exhale it out. Take another deep breath in, hold, and exhale it out. One more time, take a nice, deep final cleansing breath in, hold for 3 seconds, and exhale it all out. Pause. Take a moment to reflect on what you just experienced. Sit with your eyes closed for 30 seconds more. Then open your eyes.

It's Your Turn NOW!

How do you feel? Take a moment to write down anything that you recall that most resonated with you. Whatever it was, it is time to take action now.

As you silently read the last few passages of this book, I want you to honor your completion of what you just experienced. You needed this time. I am glad you did this, and I want you to repeat this exercise without reading the book at another time to be fully engaged and present in the process. Feel free to obtain an audio-digital copy of this book so that you can repeat this exercise by going to www.sarahreneelangley.com .

*It is your turn now. Take it.*

# **Bonus Secret Chapter**

*"You will begin to heal when you let go of the past hurts, forgive those who have wronged you, and learn to forgive yourself for your mistakes."*
**Anonymous-From relatably.com**

Now you are ready for the 8th Secret to start your new beginning.

Surprise!

This is my bonus chapter I give to you. I leave you with this one word, *Forgive.* Forgive everyone. Then say these words to yourself as you picture the offenders of your life in front of you:

*Thank you for sharing whatever you have shared with me. I allowed what you said or advised me to serve my life in the capacity it had by my choice. But I will no longer allow that to serve me, and by that, I let it go and replace it with what I want to serve in my life right now. I forgive and release you with all my heart, mind, and soul, as you only meant what was best for me. I am moving on, happy, fulfilled, and at peace.*

**Now say this loudly,** *"It's My Turn Now! I'm Taking it!"*

# It's Your Turn NOW!

If necessary, take a deep breath in, hold, and exhale it all out.

And *celebrate*! You are bringing completion to your journey. It is within us as human beings to celebrate victories! It is part of our being and essence that we tend to skip over. Take as much time as you need to celebrate your victory. Celebrate the letting go of your past. Celebrate not that you survived, but that you thrive *Right Now*! You were given key components, and while they may not make sense to you at this very moment, whatever came up for you during this process yields the potential to change the course of your life for the better. You are much further along now than you were before. You may not be where you want to be, but you are not where you used to be, that's for sure.

Wait! There's one more person to forgive. You know you need to forgive *Yourself*. Go to a mirror or pull out a mirror and take a good look at yourself. Know that it is ok to cry. Crying is soothing and healing, and quite therapeutic. Tears speak when we verbally cannot.

Take a really good look at yourself. You are beautiful. You are extraordinary. You are significant. *You matter.* You are not a fake. You are very real. You are loveable. You are forgivable. Please reframe these statements and say them aloud using "I" right now. I will wait.

Make this process personal. What you are doing is not based on how you feel, but it is based on what you speak into existence. Belief comes by hearing it over and over and over. This is my charge to you. I charge you to make this your ritual every single day for the rest of your entire life. Say this Right Now:

*I forgive myself. I am forgiven. I am sorry for not respecting myself and expecting others to respect me. I am sorry for not showing myself the same courtesy and standard that I have shown others in my life. I am sorry that I have been imbalanced and taking on everyone else's responsibilities instead of sharing responsibilities and asking for help.*

*Even though I know how my family is, and how my job/career can be, they were only going off of the script that we all generated. I declare that I am changing the script Now! I am rewriting the story of my life Now! I forgive myself for the choices I made that I was a shamed for. I forgive myself. I forgive myself for feeling like I failed. I forgive myself for wasting time and playing small. I forgive myself, Right Now!*

**Now say this loudly**, *I forgive myself now because It's My Turn Now! I'm Taking it!*

Now, with exuberance and big praise, take a long deep breath in that fills your diaphragm up, hold for 3 seconds, and let that air all out. Now jump up and down and Shout in Victory! Sing, and Dance! It's your Birthday! You were once dead, but now alive! You were also asleep, but now awake! My Mom used to say, *"Look Alive!"* as to mean, wake up. I say *Be Alive,* and take your rightful place in life today!

Now, hand me your *faux hat*! I didn't forget about this hat! That is the fake hat that you wore like a shield or mask. You do not need that fake hat because there's nothing cheap about you! You are not a cheap imitation; you are truly a designer's original! No more pretending to be a *Pretty Mask*. You are a full, actual, and a Real Self, Now Baby! Celebrate in that! You are no longer stuck, depleted, fragmented, scattered, fractured, or broken at all! Again, it's not based on feeling, but it is based on what you speak. I want you to always speak opposite of how you feel when you feel down and out. Speak life over yourself. It takes practice, but it is well worth it!

You are healed, delivered, forgiven, set free, whole, complete, purposeful, full of life, free, at peace, happy, successful, significant, outstanding, well put together, hot, on fire, wonderful, jubilant, prosperous, successful...feel free to add whatever words you want to this run on sentence! Declare that you will live a full and rich, balanced, and centered life, and that you will never ever neglect yourself again! Promise that you will do more for yourself than getting your hair and nails done to feel good! You are going to treat yourself on dates, take yourself out, and love yourself to life! Make room for yourself and these exercises in your schedule on your calendar, and commit to doing the exercises in this book on a regular basis. If you have too much on your plate and can't see how to add this to your schedule, then take inventory on what you can toss off your plate. Assess if it is hurting you or serving you, and go from there. If you need any accountability and assistance to sustain all that you have learned, feel free to review my exclusive Dynamo Diamonds program at www.sarahreneelangley.com.

*Make you your ultimate priority right now!*

# Conclusion

It is Your Turn Now to take advantage of the endless possibilities ahead of you. You do not realize that your unique gifts and natural talent coupled with your passion and action create endless happiness and success. Happiness lies in doing what you love. Doing what you love results in great success. The money is merely a by-product, and not the sole reason to pursue happiness or success. In other words, you would be surprised at how much more money you could make by choosing to do something that you love, that you are excited about, that makes a significant impact, and comes effortless for you. You have every opportunity to create a life worth living. Choose to follow your passions, and the success will follow.

*Note:* Please know that nothing changes overnight. While you may have had a breakthrough, you know more about living life on Other People's Terms than you do on Your Own Terms. Therefore, acknowledge, embrace, and accept this fact. Be patient if you don't get a breakthrough. It may be challenging to totally shift and change your entire environment. If making such a significant change causes you anxiety or depression, then *Don't!* Seek my services to help you deal with your emotions and feelings. Feel free to go to my website www.sarahreneelangley.com and learn how I can help you through my Precious Pearls Program.

Quick Story: I'd like to tell you about Kerry, a woman and mother of 2 young girls who gave up her career to move in and take care of her ailing father. She came to me because she was overwhelmed. Her partner and siblings were off living their lives and she was taking on *all* the responsibilities. After talking with her, I concluded that she was putting her life on hold and living a life split in half! Her wish was to be there for her father, and her fear was her inability to truly live her life and take care of her own obligations.

I challenged her wish and fear by asking her what life would look like if she wasn't caring for dad anymore. She exclaimed, *"I refuse to not care for my dad!"* *"Is that selfish of me if I were to not care for him?"* I told her no, because she cannot live two lives. I further explained she could no longer live the roles and responsibilities of a daughter if it goes against her life as a mother who aspires to have a career and to provide a better life for her and her children. She needed to find balance. She agreed. I helped her reframe her perspective to see her life having a great relationship with her dad, delegating responsibilities, asking for help from her siblings, and having time to get back to her career while caring for her daughters. She thought that would be too good to be true and darn near impossible! But after helping her through my Perfect Platinum Breakthrough Session, she was able to reframe her mindset and start the reframe for change in her life. Feel free to see testimonials about my services at www.sarahreneelangley.com .

The point I want to stress is to dream big and believe that the impossible is possible. There is always as solution. By making minor adjustments, Kerry was able to reframe her situation, ask for what she needed and started taking steps towards her goal. By allowing herself to see the future she wanted, she was able to create a plan that allowed her future to be a reality for herself.

You have been running around the bases, and found yourself stuck at 3$^{rd}$ base, one base short of a home run. You may know how to hit homeruns as a mother, wife, significant other, business woman, and as a career woman. But have you really hit homeruns? Where have you honestly struck out and felt like you could not tell a soul? *It is time for you to make home runs, especially for yourself now.* Know that you have all the necessary tools within to be happy and successful. You are in charge of your life and can decide which way you want it to go. Just be devoted, focused, and committed to your happiness and success.

**I leave this with you, and if you ever need me, I am**

**here for you**:

*You are not worthless, you are priceless. Your mistakes and mishaps don't define you, they refine you. You may not be Perfect, but You Are Human, and that's ok. Why? Because, you are imperfectly perfect. Be your own best friend. You are enough. The answer to your happiness and success is not out there, it's in there. Give yourself permission to be happy and successful. Remember, you are the missing link to your own equation. Let it all fall. Forgive others and yourself.*

**It's Your Turn Now. Live Life On Your Own Terms.**

# Notes

1. Maya Angelou Quote

   http://www.goodreads.com/quotes/40630-when-you-learn-teach-when-you-get-give

2. Madame CJ Walker story

   www.notablebiographies.com/Tu-We/Walker-Madame-C-J.html

3. JK Rowling Success story

   http://femaleentrepreneurassociation.com/2011/12/the-story-of-jk-rowling/

   http://www.dailymail.co.uk/home/event/article-2474863/JK-Rowling-I-poor-possible-be.html

4. Fashion Designer Tory Burch

   http://www.babson.edu/news-events/events/commencement/2014-recap/Pages/burch-tory.aspx

5. Mary Kay Quote

   https://www.goodreads.com/author/quotes/24453.Mary_Kay_Ash

6.  Oscar winner, Halle Berry's success story

    http://www.contactmusic.com/halle-berry/news/halle-lived-in-homeless-shelter_1025019

7.  The story of Anita Roddick from The Body Shop

    http://www.thebodyshop-usa.com/about-us/about_thebodyshop.aspx

8.  The success story of Sheila Marcelo

    https://www.alumni.hbs.edu/stories/Pages/story-bulletin.aspx?num=3985

9.  Arianna Huffington's success story

    http://www.success.com/article/arianna-huffington-pushing-the-limits

10. Rae Smith Quote

    https://www.pinterest.com/explore/falling-apart-quotes/

11. Missing Link Quote

    https://www.pinterest.com/pin/228487381070911970/

12. Ray Stevens lyrics

    http://www.lyricsreg.com/lyrics/ray+stevens/Be+Your+Own+Best+Friend/

It's Your Turn NOW!

13. Forgiveness Quote

http://www.relatably.com/q/bible-quotes-about-

forgiveness-of-the-past

# Resources

**DeStress To Success Group Coaching Program**
Is a 90-day Group Coaching Program that identifies barriers to success, clarifies what stress is and how to eliminate stress, and provide assessments and tools on how to become happy and successful in your career and home life. The program includes: 2x per month, 90-minute Zoom Calls, Collaborative Facebook Membership Group, Accountability Check ins by Dr. Sarah on Mondays, Member-Only Section with Done-For-You tools and templates, 1 Bonus Precious Pearl Session, and Deep Discounts to Live Events, Spa Retreats, and other LeadHer Membership Programs.
http://sarahreneelangley.com/coaching-membership-programs/

**Perfect Platinum LeadHer Elite Coaching Program**
Is a 12-month program exclusively for executive and entrepreneurial women seeking mentorship, accountability, and support to rejuvenate in their leadership, productivity, and performance. It includes: A Jump Start VIP Session, Effective Business and Leadership Success Strategies, DeStress to Success Self-Care Tips, Personal Accountability and Access to Dr. Sarah weekly for an entire year. Additionally, you will receive 90 minute, bi-monthly sessions with Dr. Sarah, the Gorgeous Gold Membership Package, 1 ticket to Dr. Sarah's Spa Retreat, VIP Access

and Meals to Dr. Sarah's Live Events for you and a guest, and VIP Access to other Amazing Events with Dr. Sarah! You will receive Dr. Sarah's forthcoming book, 1 Precious Pearl Session, and Certificate of Completion.

http://sarahreneelangley.com/coaching-membership-programs/

**Dynamo Diamond LeadHer Mastery Coaching Program**
Is a 6-month program exclusively for executive and entrepreneurial women seeking mentorship, accountability, and support to reinvent themselves by pursuing their purpose and passion. It includes: A Jump Start VIP Session, Effective Business and Leadership Success Strategies, DeStress to Success Self-Care Tips, Personal Accountability and Access to Dr. Sarah weekly for 6 months. You will receive 60 minute, bi-monthly sessions with Dr. Sarah, VIP Access and Meals to Dr. Sarah's Live Events for you and a guest, and VIP Access to to other Amazing Events with Dr. Sarah! You will receive Dr. Sarah's forthcoming book, 1 Precious Pearl Session, and Certificate of Completion.

http://sarahreneelangley.com/coaching-membership-programs/

**Precious Pearls LeadHer Exclusive Coaching Program**
Is a program that is purchased as a package of sessions exclusively for executive and entrepreneurial women seeking emotional and

mental support due to challenges impacting their work, home, and social life. This program is for women in need of restoration through self-care and life balance systems.  It includes: Marriage, Family, and Relationship Coaching, DeStress to Success Self-Care Tips, Time and Stress Management Strategies, and Leadership, Assertiveness, and Communication Consulting. Sessions are 30-45 minutes and scheduled accordingly.  You will also receive Dr. Sarah's forthcoming book, and Certificate of Completion.
http://sarahreneelangley.com/coaching-membership-programs/

### Gorgeous Gold Membership

This membership includes a subscription to Dr. Sarah's Monthly LeadHer Today Newsletter, access to Dr. Sarah's Facebook Membership Group, and Inspirational and Motivational Quotes and Messages.  Additionally, you can submit questions to Ask Dr. Sarah Column, where Dr. Sarah will provide responses to your questions in the next issue, and you will be part of the Dr. Sarah's Space Monthly Q and A Zoom Sessions. You will have Monday Accountability Check Ins with Dr. Sarah via the Facebook Group, plus access to Dr. Sarah's Member-Only audio library and recorded webinars, plus Done-For-You homework templates and assignments. Lastly, you will receive deep discounts on Dr. Sarah's future live events and on products, programs, and services.

It's Your Turn NOW!

http://sarahreneelangley.com/coaching-membership-programs/

### Sexy Silver Membership

This membership includes a subscription to Dr. Sarah's Monthly LeadHer Today Newsletter, and Inspirational and Motivational Quotes and Messages. Additionally, you can submit questions to Ask Dr. Sarah Column, where Dr. Sarah will provide responses to your questions in the next issue, and you will be part of Dr. Sarah's Space Monthly Q and A Zoom Sessions. You will also be eligible to upgrade to the Gorgeous Gold Membership as a limited time offer.

http://sarahreneelangley.com/coaching-membership-programs/

### Beautiful Bronze Membership

This membership includes a subscription to Dr. Sarah's Monthly LeadHer Today Newsletter, and Inspirational and Motivational Quotes and Messages. Additionally, you can submit questions to Ask Dr. Sarah Column, where Dr. Sarah will provide responses to your questions in the next issue. You will be eligible to upgrade to either the Silver or Gold Membership as a limited time offer.

http://sarahreneelangley.com/coaching-membership-programs/

**Products**

To view products, including preordering Dr. Sarah's forthcoming books, ***Just Get Naked! Accepting and Embracing The True Skin You're In,*** and, ***From Career Woman to Caregiver, Parenting the Parent: An Autobiography,*** our Lady LeadHER tee shirts, LeadHer Notebook, LeadHer Bookmarkers, Dr. Sarah's Inspirational Posters, and LeadHer Tote Bags, please go to www.sarahreneelangley.com .

**DeStress To Success Quiz**

This Free Quiz assesses your stressor profile type to determine the causes to your stressful life. The quiz also includes tips and recommendations on how to eliminate your stress so that you can inevitably be happier and more successful in your business, career, and home life. Discover your unique stress profile and the key steps to eliminating stress now! https://sarahreneelangley.leadpages.co/destress-to-success/

# SMART and SIMPLE Goals

Being the resourceful person that I am, I wanted to leave you with some additional resources that will help you solidify all that you have learned and to do what Berny Dohrmann had said the Foreword. He stated for you to, *"Make notes in the book of future things to do, and make a list of what you are committing to do to make it your turn Now."* Now that you have explored what happiness and success look like for you, identified the necessary steps to take action on your happiness and success, and reframed your mindset to go after your happy and success just for you, you will need to manage your sustainability for continual happiness and success. You can either go about this strategy SMART or SIMPLE, which are acronyms to help remember how to do your goals effectively. Let's explore in depth my first resource for you, SMART and SIMPLE goals.

# SMART Goals

Smart is an acronym for **S**pecific, **M**easurable, **A**ttainable, **R**elevant, and **T**ime Conscious. Before starting any goal, you want to have a plan, or what I tell my clients, a *Course of Action*. Having a course of action establishes the foundation or blueprint to what you are going after. When working toward any goal, make sure it answers the following questions: *Who, What, When, Where, Why,* and *How*.

**Specific.** *Specific* means to be concise and exact on what it is that you are trying to accomplish. Let's use this example: *I want to lose weight.* You have the goal in mind, but the goal is too vague and general. Making it specific would sound like this: *I want to lose 10 inches from my waist.*

See the difference? You specified who's doing it and what you're doing. We will now go to the *M*.

**Measurable.** *Measurable* means to have the ability to track, assess, and calculate your course of action. Having mini goals or objectives toward your main goal helps to measure your progress. Back to our example: *I want to lose 10 inches off my*

160

*waist by: 1. Eating small portions 3 times a day, 7 days a week.*
*2. Going to the gym for 1/2 hour, 5 times a week. 3. Doing a*
*daily log at least 2 times a day for the next 90 days to track*
*progress.*

So, now you have the *who*, *what*, *where*, and *how*. Now going
to *A*.


**Attainable.** *Attainable* means setting goals that are
achievable. Make goals that will be easy to attain: *I will lose 10*
*inches from my waist. I will lose 1-2 inches in 90 days.*
This is as opposed to saying that I will lose 10 inches in 10 days,
which would be highly impossible, not to mention unhealthy.
You want goals that will be attainable, not drastic and possibly
costly to your health. Let's move to *R*.


**Realistic.** *Realistic* means making your goals realistic.
Make them attainable and relevant to you. Do not base your
goals on someone else's goals. Someone else may be able to
lose 10 inches from his or her waist in 10 days because of their
metabolism, and you may have to go about losing inches a

different way. It is entirely okay. Do what make sense for you so that it doesn't affect your overall way of life and well-being.

*Therefore, I want to lose 10 inches from my waist by losing 1-2 inches a month through changing my diet and the way I diet. For the first week I will eat smaller portions at least once in the week. During the 2nd week, I will eat smaller portions, at least 2 times per week, and for the 3rd week, I will eat 3 smaller portions, etc. By the end of month, I will eat smaller portions at least 5 times a week.*

See the difference? You are breaking it down instead of quitting cold turkey! Don't shock your body by making drastic moves from what it is accustomed. Make realistic moves. Take the goal apart to determine who's doing it, what you're doing, when you're doing it, and how you're doing it. Let's go to the last letter, *T*.

**Time Conscious.** *Time-Conscious* means completing your goals in a timely manner. Two things you do not want to do are set unrealistic time components, or set time so far out that you are not challenged or accountable to accomplish them. For example, an unrealistic time component is when you set a goal stating that you will quit smoking forever in one week when you have smoked for 25 years. An example of setting a goal too far in advance is you will stop eating chocolate by January 2020 (exaggeration, but still you are nowhere near being challenged to begin quitting the 'chocolate habit'). Set a timeframe that is challenging and holds you accountable: *I will lose 10 inches off my waist starting January 1st, 2016 and end by 9/1/2016.*

Now, put the entire S.M.A.R.T. goal together and it comes out like this: *I want to lose 10 inches from my waist by 9/1/2016. I will accomplish this by losing 1-2 inches a month for the next 9 months. I will do this by: 1.) Eating smaller portions; 2.) Going to the gym 5 times a week. In one month, I will increase smaller portions weekly, up to 2 of 3 meals daily. I will track my progress weekly. I will check my status every 3 months up to 9/1/2016.*

This covers the parameters of who's doing it, what you're doing, when you are doing it, where you are doing it, and how you are doing it. It also covers the why, which is to be healthier and improved. Note: If you do not meet your goal, go back to the example: *I will lose 1-2 inches in the first 3 months*, then assess the *why* and the *what*. Reflect on why you did not lose the inches, and what in your plan didn't work. *Do not* give up *or* quit! Simply readjust your course of action and resume. Simplify the way you do things and contour those goals to fit you.

Remember, do not give up or quit, but simply readjust or make your goals SIMPLE to have a future full of happiness and success just for you! Let's discuss SIMPLE goals.

# SIMPLE Goals

SIMPLE goals, developed by Rick Torben, stands for **S**et **E**xpectations, **I**nvite Commitment, **M**easure Progress, **P**rovide Feedback, **L**ink to Consequences, and **E**valuate Effectiveness. SIMPLE goals were designed for managers to use for their employees, but I do not see why we can't use this to apply towards your own happiness and success goals.

**Set Expectations.** Set your focus, time, energy, and resources toward attaining your happiness and success. Be clear on your own expectations so as not to set yourself up for failure and disappointment. Be realistic and make your goals feasible to attain. Going back to the example of losing weight, if your expectation is to realistically lose 10 pounds in one month, rearrange your life accordingly, i.e. join a weight and dieting club or group, sign up to join a gym, lessen the trips to the ice cream parlor, etc. Do not expect to lose 10 pounds if you do not change anything contrary to what you have been doing that caused you to gain weight in the first place. Set your expectations of yourself, be clear about them, and show the courtesy of giving yourself permission to follow through on them. Of course, have a weight journal to notate your journey, paying attention to any self-talk, resistance, feelings, behaviors, and actions. Notate any external distractions, like family, friends, and business, that may actually play against you in accomplishing your goals. You are shifting in your life, and everyone in your life are comfortable with you remaining the same. But you are not comfortable, and that is why you are giving yourself permission to take your turn now and making this necessary shift.

**Invite Commitment.** Commit to achieving your goals. You may have been very committed to everything else in your life, even committed to being successful. But that does not mean it translates or will transfer over to a commitment for this new personal goal of happiness and success for yourself. Please write in your *Happiness and Success Journal* how accomplishing these goals will benefit you personally, and how it will benefit others. But the focus should really be on how it benefits you; you have already done things that directly

166

benefited others and indirectly benefited yourself. It is time for this goal to primarily, and even solely, benefit you in order to fully understand what it is to be happy and successful for yourself, *unapologetically, and guiltlessly.* Give yourself permission to feel good at having this goal being all about you. Additionally, create a way to hold yourself accountable. I will address this later when we get to **L** of SIMPLE.

**Measure Progress.** Create a performance measure to track your progress so that you can determine if you are meeting your goals or not. Instead of being disappointed that you haven't lost 10 pounds in three months, review and assess your performance measure to see the steps you have taken in your attempt to complete this goal. In other words, in reviewing the steps made, like, *going to the gym 5 days a week, or going to the ice cream parlor only once a week instead of your normal 5 times weekly,* you were able to see that for two months you sporadically went to the gym twice a week and you actually increased going to the ice cream parlor six days a week during a 2-month period! You can visually see where you may have deviated from your plan, where you fell off the wagon, and where you can tweak your steps to successfully complete your goals. Writing about what happened in your Happiness and Success Journal will also make a world of difference in a few ways. First, you can turn this into a book for others to know how to become happy and successful. Second, you can refer back to your journal when you face other challenges and see how you were able to triumph and overcome past challenges. Lastly, you have a standard to create future goals.

**Provide Feedback.** As mentioned in explaining the **M** in SIMPLE, providing feedback regarding your thoughts, feelings, and behavior is crucial because you can explore its source of creation. Your behavior during this process of pursuing happiness and success for yourself may be noteworthy as it may tell a lot about whether it is the same behavior that was modeled, or if it is a result of your upbringing. Perhaps your mom tried to be happy and attempted to lose weight to feel better about herself, but she self-sabotaged because your dad subconsciously wanted your mom to be a certain weight so that she would feel self-conscious about herself and go to your dad for comfort and support. She knew that was really the only way she would depend on him for support and comfort during her journey, so she inevitably stopped her attempts to lose weight so that the dynamic of their relationship remain unscathed. Explore if there are similar undertones in your current relationship with your significant other or with others.

**Link to Consequences.** This is my favorite SIMPLE goal! Why you ask? We are motivated by rewards and consequences. We have learned to be this way ever since we were young. I learned not to do what my brothers did in order to avoid punishment. They received enough whippings for all of us! I witnessed which behaviors were rewarded, and which behaviors received punishment. I would like for you to create a behavior and thinking chart. Write down all of the good thoughts, self-sabotaging thoughts, and actions that lead you to your happiness and success, and also list the good thoughts, self-sabotaging thoughts, and behaviors that take you off course. Once you list them, then you can create a daily chart for these items so that on a weekly basis you are tracking how you are doing. Going back to the losing weight example, if you plan to lose 10 pounds in three months, then at the end of each month you would look to see how well you have progressed. If you, let's say, lost 5 pounds at the end of the month and that was your mini-goal within the main goal, then *Celebrate and Reward Yourself*! Create a list of rewards that you can choose from. If you gained 5 pounds at the end of the month, then link the consequence to it. If that means no cell phone for a week except for emergencies. (I would be careful what you classify as emergencies so that you don't cheat and use the cell phone for the emergency to call your friend about the latest issue that happened on *The Real Housewives of Orange County*!) It is about maturity and discipline, and if you do not deserve to celebrate your mini successes because you did not meet your goal so far, then you need to have a consequence that you know will propel you to do better next time.

**Case Study: Me**

It's Your Turn NOW!

I once worked in medical records for a teen summer program called Phil-a-Job in Philadelphia when I was 16. It was my very first professional job, and it was the very first time I was fired! I think it had something to do with my not doing my job as expected. While I had the job, I put a gold ring with my middle name, Renee, on a lay-away plan. I would go to the jewelry store every two weeks to pay off the ring. I had a goal in mind, and that was to have my ring by the end of the summer. But I didn't do my job as expected, and as a consequence I was fired. You'd think I would have learned from this over the years because I mentioned earlier I was fired and laid off so many times! I talked my way into getting my job back and I worked harder than ever. I finally purchased my ring, and I was so happy! When I received my job back, I was motivated to do my job as intended and better than anyone else, which I did. I gave it the respect that the job deserved, and the reward was the respect of the staff, who threw me a party when the summer job ended. The best homemade carrot cake ever! Plus, I was able to wear my beautiful *Renee* ring to the party! Make sure you link your rewards and consequences to your goals of happiness and success so that you can stay on track and fulfil all your goals. Finally, we come to the **E** in SIMPLE goals.

**Evaluate Effectiveness.** Review, assess, and analyze how your journey has been regarding your goals toward happiness and success. As mentioned earlier, notate all that has worked and that has resulted in the fulfilment of your goals, and then discard what has not worked. In other words, *take in the meat and spit out the bones.* Ever heard that before? For the sake of the point, the meat is the best part, the part that nourishes and helps us become strong. Therefore, take in what works for your happiness and success and get rid of what doesn't work. Do not make the mistake of copying others' ways of accomplishing goals. What worked for others may not work for you.

I remember telling my couples during relationship counseling and in my retreats that instead of patterning after their parents' marriage, they should only take bits and pieces that they would like to apply to their own marriage. I encouraged them to seize their greatest opportunity in recreating their own style of marriage. Many of them were happy and thankful for this tip on creating change and doing things differently.  Likewise, write down what works for you and what doesn't work for you with regards to obtaining your happiness and success. Then, turn it into a how to book and publish it later on, and then watch it become a best seller! You will be amazed at how your own unique story will significantly impact and make a difference for those going through the same things as you are right now. Trust me.

# Happiness and Success Story: Mary Nelson Langley

I would love to share my second resource which is my Mom's success story. I would totally be remiss if I didn't add this as another resource of encouragement and inspiration for you.

My Mom was a dynamo diamond when it came to caring for her family and other families in our neighborhood. She desired to go to college but her parents could not afford to send her. After graduation from high school, she was sent by her parents to live in Philadelphia to care for her sister's children. Then she put most of her children through college over the years, and worked in the Philadelphia school system as a teacher's aide helping those with special needs. One day, she registered to attend Philadelphia Community College. It took her 19 years to finish her Associate Degree in Elementary Education. She had taken one class each semester, had stopped attending classes to care for family, and then resumed, and finally finished. My Dad would joke and question why she even attended college; he didn't finish school since he had to stop attending after 6$^{th}$ grade to care for his grandmother and great grandmother. There may have been times that she wanted to stop attending college because her husband didn't agree or thought it was unnecessary for her to go to college. However, her belief system, her lifelong desire to go to college, and seeing her kids attending college, all propelled her to finish. It may have been challenging and it may have taken a long time, but she finished right around the time when she was diagnosed with early onset Alzheimer's Disease.

I decided to share that titbit to say, had she stopped pursuing her happiness, then she would have inevitably missed out on it. Thank God she didn't. Think about that as you reflect on the challenges and the rewards of being happy and successful by accomplishing your goals. Mom knew it would change the dynamic between Dad and her, but she decided to pursue her lifelong dream anyway and, guess what, despite Dad deflecting her getting the degree because of his own stuff—please let me repeat this—*his own stuff, and not her stuff*—Mom finished school and their relationship inevitably changed. He stopped deflecting and saying anything against her having a degree after a while, and he did support her at her graduation. I have pics to show for it! Overall, he was proud of his wife, and is supportive of her to this day, even in her late stages of Alzheimer's Disease, having been together for over 50 years.

The point I am making to you is this, give yourself permission to be happy and successful. Accept the fact that things may change, but that's ok! It is for *your* happiness and success. Put more value and weight on the fact that dealing with challenges, which by the way is inevitable to happen because that is life, does not mean that it is the end of the world because you decided to do one thing that makes you happy for a change! *Do It for You*! For over 50 years, Dad has witnessed his meek, very quiet, and shy wife persevere through adversity, bore his children, cared for him, their family, and others, and despite all the odds, fulfilled her lifelong dream before it was too late. There is honor in that, for sure. And if my mommy can successfully go after her dreams, so can you. Take heed to the example she has provided. I have, and it works!

Overall, please explore and write down your thoughts, feelings, and behaviors in your Happiness and Success Journal to see what holds you back from going after your happiness and success. Additionally, be honest with yourself as you trace back its sources of being held back and stuck so that you can then position yourself for change to successfully fulfil your goals.

SARAH RENEE LANGLEY

# Conversations About Your Happiness and Success

Here is my final resource for you. I want to leave you with an experience I have had that totally changed my life forever, and helped me inevitably start the process of writing this book.

**What are Conversations?**

After attending the my very first Millionaire Mind Intensive with my organization, New Peaks, I have learned some things about my conversations concerning money. It blew me away to discover my internal and external conversations, which were comprised of my *beliefs, attitudes, values, and feelings,* about money. I did not realize that I fooled myself into thinking that I was financially successful because I owned my own home, car, business, and had obtained a PhD. Yet, I sabotaged myself to the point that, while my business made six figures, my income was lower than what my parents made in one year when they were working!

**Blue Collar Vs. White Collar**

I remember when my Dad connected me with someone at his company to interview for an administrative assistant position. He had been a janitor with the company for over 30 years, and I had just graduated from college with my Master's Degree. I went to the interview, and I bombed. *On purpose, too.* I did not know why I did that. But I now realized why. I could not bear to see my Dad come to my desk and ask for my trash. It made me sad and tearful to think that the man who raised me had a meagre blue collar job compared to my future white collar job. So subconsciously, I sabotaged the interview and did not get the job. Also, I grew up hearing, *it is better to be poor than to be rich because rich people are stingy and selfish.* I subconsciously sabotaged myself regarding my financial success, *until now.*

**What Are Your Conversations?**

In sharing my example, I want you to explore not your conversations regarding money, but your conversations about being happy and successful. We tend to gravitate toward tangible evidence in a more biased matter, and accept the evidence that is consistent with our own views. In other words, we need money to buy things, yes or yes? I can look at my life and say that I didn't really need money to make me happy, and my justification is evident in my upbringing. I can say that I grew up in a loving household full of great memories, yet we were poor. I can justify that families who come from rich households tend to be miserable as reported on television or evidenced in reality shows. I am justifying that being broke equates to being happy, and being rich equates to being unhappy. The funny thing about this concept is, why was I unhappy when I thought being broke was supposed to equal to being happy, especially when I get to Heaven? I had to really explore my internal conversations regarding money, happiness, and success. I implore you to do the same.

**Steps to Explore Your Conversations**

What are your conversations about being happy and successful? Is being happy and successful just a fantasy? Is being happy and successful unattainable in your mind and, therefore, you settle with what you have accomplished so far? Do you justify having cared for your family, raised your children, having a great job, and making lots of money as being happy and successful? Are you truly happy? Please write down in your Happiness and Success Journal your beliefs, attitudes, values, feelings, and behaviors as they relate to your happiness and success so as to address these and make appropriate changes where necessary.

Afterwards, you will be more aware and honest with yourself so that you can prevent self-sabotaging and increase your chances to finally being happy and even more successful than ever. Be on a mission to being happy and successful for *You*!

*I congratulate you wholeheartedly, and cannot wait to here all the success stories you will have about your happiness and your success. Feel free to share them at www.sarahreneelangley.com.*

*Amen.*

181

## More Books From

     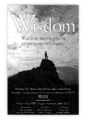  

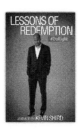     

    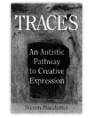

    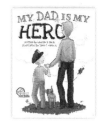

Your

Book

Here

# www.PerfectPublishing.com